THE CHURCH, POLITICS,
AND SOCIETY

The Church, Politics, and Society

Dialogues on Current Problems

by
JAMES A. PIKE
and
JOHN W. PYLE

MOREHOUSE-GORHAM COMPANY
New York
1955

Printed in the United States of America
By The Haddon Craftsmen, Inc., Scranton, Pa.

TO

OUR COLLEAGUES ON THE CHAPTER

OF THE

CATHEDRAL OF ST. JOHN THE DIVINE

EDWARD N. WEST   HOWARD A. JOHNSON

DARBY W. BETTS   GEORGE W. TORSNEY

PREFACE

THE Biblical view of history shares with the secularist doctrine of progress the expectation that the possibilities of *good* will increase as the generations unfold. But more profoundly than the secularist view, the Biblical view knows that the possibilities of evil likewise increase. Thus it should not surprise the Christian that the problems of the world are greater than ever before and the consequences of decision have greater magnitude.

Thus there has been no time when the Church was more called upon to bring the Light with which it is entrusted to bear upon the issues of the day. And in good measure that is what it is doing—on many fronts at once. The Church has been just active enough and inactive enough to bring upon it, paradoxically enough, a double critique: that it is too much concerned with political and social questions and that it is not concerned enough. These challenges are being pressed more insistently today than ever before, and there is a continuing dialogue going on between spokesmen for the Churches and critics of the right and the left. Thus it seemed to us that the issues might be better aired through the dialogue method than through straight, essay presentation. In this approach we do not use the critic merely as a foil, or "straw man." Since we stand in a Christian tradition which views the Church as under judgment, we believe that some of the most

7

important things on the subjects at hand are being said by the Church's critics, and this conviction is herein reflected.

The book is based on the script of eleven dialogues presented by the authors last summer over the ABC radio network under the auspices of the National Council of the Churches of Christ in the U.S.A., some of which were also presented at Sunday Evensong in the Cathedral of St. John the Divine, New York City. We wish to express our thanks to those who collaborated in the planning: The Reverend Dr. Roswell Barnes, Associate General Secretary of the National Council of the Churches of Christ in the U.S.A.; Mr. Ben Wilbur, radio director of its broadcasting and Film Commission; Mr. William J. Moll, director of public relations for the Bishop and the Cathedral; and Miss Ruth Trexler, then manager of religious and educational activities, American Broadcasting Company. We also are grateful to the many listeners who wrote expressing appreciation and constructive criticism. We wish to express our thanks also to those who typed the scripts: Mrs. Dorothy Fry, Mrs. Dale Eshleman, and Mrs. Lillian Cromey.

These dialogues follow the precedent of the previous summer's discussions by one of us with the Reverend Dr. John McG. Krumm, Chaplain of Columbia University, issued by the same publisher as the 1954 Bishop of New York Book under the title *Roadblocks to Faith*. The latter was concerned with apologetics, i.e., the reasoned commendation of the Christian faith to the secular mind. Different as the theme of this present work is, it too is apologetics, since both the very fact of the Church's witness against the great evils of our time and the relevance and soundness of the Christian answer to pressing problems are among the most convincing reasons for heeding the Church's Gospel—as has been testified to by many latter-day converts from secularism whom the authors have had the privilege of counseling. In its public positions no less than in its worship, its corporate life, and its pastoral care of individuals, the Church is called upon to demonstrate the saving truth

of the theme of the World Council of Churches at Evanston:
Christ the Hope of the World.

Cathedral House   J. A. P.
New York City   J. W. P.
Michaelmas, 1954

WOE to the inhabiters of the earth and of the sea!
for the devil is come down unto you, having great
wrath, because he knoweth that he hath but a short
time.

—from the Epistle for Michaelmas

CONTENTS

The Church, Politics, and Society

CHAPTER ONE

"Shouldn't the Church stay out of politics entirely and just concern itself with making individuals better?"

CRITIC: I don't go to church very often, but I'm a bit concerned as to the kind of sermons I hear when I do go. Last time I went, for instance, the preacher was talking about bad housing conditions in the cities; the time I went before that, he was denouncing the methods of Congressional investigating committees.

Exponent: And so?

Critic: Well, I'm concerned about the fact that the Church has been indulging more and more in statements about politics, economics, and social matters of all sorts. I wonder if this is really the kind of thing that's going to help me as an individual. When I turn to the Church I want help for the things that are bothering me. I want a certain amount of comfort. I want some inspiration. The Church being in politics is certainly not going to do this for me. Should the Church be in politics?

Exponent: First of all, I'd like to agree with you as to your right to expect from the Church personal help and comfort and inspiration and guidance. And whatever else the Church ought to stand for in the world, it must never neglect that task. I think it's only fair to say that as the Church has more and more concerned itself with larger issues, it has not seemed to neglect ministering to individuals. And it is even improving in the best ways of meeting the needs of individuals.

Critic: But one of the things I do not need or want from the Church is direction as to how I should vote. It's the Church's business to help me spiritually, not politically.

Exponent: You're right there. The Church should not tell you how to vote. Nor should the Church tell you what particularly proposed law will be best for us, and, certainly, the Church should never announce that such-and-such a solution to a problem is the will of God. But the Church must hold before men what God's will is; what the principles are which should govern a righteous society. And the Church must continue to call attention to gross abuses of human dignity and gross failure to meet human needs wherever it exists in our society.

Critic: But isn't that the job of politics or economics? These matters don't have anything to do with religion.

Exponent: I'm afraid that that statement indicates too narrow an idea of religion. The late Archbishop of Canterbury, William Temple, wisely said something to this effect: It is a great mistake to think that God is interested only, or even primarily, in religion.

Another way to get at the same thing is to define religion more broadly and to say that all the concerns that God has for His children are also the concerns of men who bear the name of Christian. Let me give you an example. Certainly you would regard it as a religious and ethical concern if a family with no roof over their head were going to have to stay out in the cold, and you had an opportunity to put them up or find them shelter.

Critic: Yes, that's exactly my point. This is dealing right with individuals and this is what the Church ought to be teaching men to do.

Exponent: Yes, I know; but if we should be concerned about families without roofs over their heads, shouldn't we take account of the realities, and be concerned for more extensive low-cost housing so that people don't find themselves in this degrading situation of having to beg a night's lodging from you, for example? Let me extend this to the matter of food. Certainly, it has always been regarded as a Christian duty to give a man a sandwich and cup of coffee if he's hungry and without the means of buying anything for himself. Now, shouldn't we, as Christians, be concerned to help create conditions that make it less likely that people will find themselves in such a condition?

Critic: But don't a great many of these things depend on technical knowledge and technical ability? The

Church, after all, is not equipped to know the facts about these things. If I want to build a house, I go to a building contractor.

Exponent: Right you are. Let's get back to my earlier point. The Church cannot give a blueprint. The Church cannot back particular politicians or particular proposals. But the Church can point out to us that a *status quo* isn't meeting the need. The Church can condemn proposals which are in their very nature against Christian principles.

Critic: Granted, then, that the Church should make some statement or take some stand on the general principles involved, doesn't this still present a problem? Because it means that the Church is going to be in a half-way position between real political action on the one hand and real spirituality on the other.

Exponent: The Church is, in a sense, in a half-way position, but I'd like to qualify a little bit this word "spirituality." Personally, I can imagine nothing more spiritual, in the best sense of the word, than guidance toward constructive solutions to the common problems of the children of God. But I agree we are in a half-way position. If we can help clarify what the issues are in the light of eternal convictions about man's destiny and meaning, then haven't we reason to hope—and, certainly, from past history we do have reason to hope —that you and others who may have particular skills, aptitudes, and special knowledge will better be able to act directly to remedy specific difficulties and develop support of particular movements?

Critic: Well, this raises another problem, and that is that there are often two or three ways of doing the same thing, or rather, there may be more than one answer to the same general problem. Are you suggesting that once the Church has made a statement or taken a stand on some general political principle, I and all my laymen friends should automatically follow the same course of specific political action?

Exponent: Not at all. We do have some reason to hope that sincere Christians will be guided by the same principles, once those principles are made evident in the light of a particular controversy or need. But different Christians will have different facts at their disposal and will differ sincerely as to the solutions.

Critic: Let's take the problem of segregation in the public schools, for instance. The facts, the place, the local circumstances may have a lot to do with the nature of the problem itself. In an area with a high proportion of Negro population, when is the right time to eliminate segregation in the public schools? Now here we have to have the facts.

Exponent: You're right in implying that the Church is not a fact-finding agency. But it's still the Church's job to make evident at all points that a segregated pattern in any part of our society is not according to the will of God. The Church may not be the best equipped agency to prescribe the exact lay of the land in a particular county in terms of the actual effect of the elimination of segregation in a given month or year. But suppose the relative percentages of the white and colored children were known, and suppose all the parties agreed that a segregated pattern was not according to the will of God; even then, sincere Christians could differ in their judgment as to whether greater harm or good would come from immediate action or from a somewhat delayed or perhaps gradual action.

Critic: If this is true, what good does it do for the Church to make any statements at all about these matters —if it cannot make a statement of fact and give actual guidance and direction to people in making the decisions they have to make in politics? Why doesn't it just stay clear of it completely?

Exponent: Well, I shall try to give you two or three reasons why the Church can't stay clear of the matter completely. First of all, Christian theology and Christian ethics are a profound body of thought which can throw a great deal of light on man's situation and man's need and this should be brought to people's minds as they are actually doing their thinking about these things. And second, because the Church does deal with the individual and his spiritual condition, it can provide inspiration for people's zeal, so that they can more ably persevere in any cause to which they devote themselves; and perhaps even more important, it brings something into their lives which, we hope, can purify their motives. As you well know, one of the difficulties about making judgments on social issues is that the interest of one's class or of one's family or of one's own personal interests so often color his judgment.

Critic: Doesn't the Church's entering the scene mean that people just differ over the facts more zealously with more religious emotion?

Exponent: Perhaps so. But that in itself is a good thing. A certain social ferment of the right sort often produces more creative solutions than merely an armchair discussion of social issues and an examination of dull statistical tables.

Critic: But hadn't the dull statistical tables—as you describe them—better be examined by the preacher before he holds himself up as a prophet?

Exponent: Yes, I agree. While the Church has a general job all the time to try to preach the principles of social ethics, prophecy means speaking out as to a given temporal situation in the light of the eternal. And since it is important that what is said be to the point and since there can be no value in the preacher's comments unless they relate to matters which are really before peoples' minds, the preacher ought to be rather avid in reading the newspapers.

Critic: You think he should believe everything he sees in the papers?

Exponent: I hope not. But I hope he has been a consistent enough observer of public affairs and has taken various means of informing himself as to situations so that he can evaluate the excellent reporting that we generally find, sufficiently to have a reasonable basis for assuming a certain factual situation to be true.

Critic: But that means the Church is getting into the realm of facts again, doesn't it?

Exponent: I'm glad you called me on that. I think there has been an apparent inconsistency in what I'm saying. Let me try again. A mother would hardly rush a child to a doctor just on the theory that something could be wrong with the child. The mother, sensitive to her children's state, would have noted fever, coughing, spots on the skin, or one thing or another. Her observation of this condition would cause her to call in the experts. So she is, in a sense, engaged in a certain factual form of medical practice—at the initiatory stage—so it would be very foolish of her to presume to be the one who gathers or passes on the facts that had to do with the prescription that's to be issued.

Critic: Now, just what's the point of this illustration?

Exponent: Simply this. The Church similarly, both in terms of its individual clergy and in terms of the various agencies of the denomination, should keep alert to the symptoms of our times and sense evil conditions or proposals—but when it comes to working out the best solutions the Church is not particularly equipped for the research called for; nor should it ever appear to bind the legitimate freedom of the Christian individual in drawing from his own experience the conclusions which should follow from the principles which the Church proclaims.

Critic: Well, I can see this in connection with the agencies and commissions of the Church which do a great amount of good work in collecting facts and informing people on various matters. I heard a preacher once, however, who stated that the Gospel for the day was a certain bill in Congress on public housing. Now, this isn't what I want to hear when I come to church.

Exponent: But if you're like most people if you don't hear the Church's views on it there, you won't hear it at all. It's a fact, perhaps an unfortunate fact, that most people don't really follow closely the reports of the various church agencies on social questions, and it's generally up to the minister to be the one that brings these facts into relationship with peoples' minds in terms of the claims of God. But as to not wanting to hear this in church, I think you've put your finger on something rather important there. It has been said that the task of preaching is to comfort the afflicted and to afflict the comfortable. People generally don't like to hear anything that challenges their own notions, particularly if these notions serve their own self-interests.

Critic: Well, come now. That's unfair. I'm just as interested as anyone in the welfare of my fellow men.

Exponent: Oh, sure, but you might sing a different tune if you were, say, a banker who owned the worst block of slums in the town and your minister felt called upon to demand action to clean up these slums to avoid multiple occupancy and to require certain improvements in the property at your expense.

Critic: I'm not so fortunate as to be a banker or own a block of buildings, but if I were and I heard a minister telling me what I ought to be doing with my business and the buildings I own, what I would say is that he doesn't know as much about my business as I do. And, furthermore, I am responsible for the decisions of that business and he isn't. I am responsible to my depositors or I have responsibility to ——

Exponent: Right here, however, is where the Church comes into this field at the deepest level. This is where the community problem and your problem overlap and the Church is interested in both. One of the things the Church has to say to people over and over again—and it has to say it to its ministers as well, I might say—is that we have a final responsibility and loyalty only to God and that our responsibility to investors or to our families or to anyone else is a secondary responsibility. In other words, the Church is trying to lift the sights of people above these immediate claims upon them. Not to the neglect of those claims, but so that the will of God may come about in society and all claims may be subordinated to His rule. Now one advantage of the fact that the Church ministers to all types of people —people in all kinds of occupations, and with all kinds of interests—is that maybe some of the banker's investors might be reached also, and they, too, would be open to the idea of yielding their own self-interests to a greater interest. The investors no less than the banker ought to be hearing something about the will of God.

Critic: Quite true. But the best way to hear about the will of God is in the Bible, isn't it? If I hear about banking in the Church instead of about the Bible, I'm not going to find out much about the will of God. There's not very much about banking in the Bible.

Exponent: Maybe not, but there's plenty in the Bible about social conditions and God's judgment upon them. Haven't you read about our Lord's running the money changers out of the Temple? The Bible is replete with condemnation by the prophets of particular evil conditions. We see Isaiah warning Ahaz, the king, against a foreign alliance—and why? Because it will compromise the principles of a nation dedicated to God. We see Elijah publicly denouncing King Ahab's methods of exercising what today we call the right of eminent domain; namely, in connection with taking Naboth's vineyard.

Critic: Ah, but what about St. Paul? He didn't seem to have any particular criticism of slavery, for instance. In the Epistle to Philemon, you can see that he tells a slave to go back to his master and he tells the master to treat the slave in certain ways. You see him dealing with the individual, not with social conditions.

Exponent: As far as St. Paul is concerned, I think this is a good illustration and I'm glad you brought up the fact that the Church itself grows in social consciousness through the continuing guidance of the Holy Spirit. It is as though a lamp is being constantly carried further and further out into the dark recesses of the world. But even if St. Paul had understood fully the evil of slavery, there wasn't a thing the Church could have done about it in those times. The Church was then simply trying to get a beachhead in the empire, and certainly in that case the first job, and perhaps the only job, was to convert people and put a new spirit in individual relations. And that's just what the purpose of the Epistle to Philemon was—it was an attempt to improve the person-to-person relationship of the slave and his master when the slave returned.

Critic: And that is just what I think the Church ought to keep on doing.

Exponent: To be sure. But, in addition, the Church cannot ignore the added responsibilities that come to it when God has prospered it and given it a larger place in the affairs of the world.

Critic: Well, isn't there a question of priority here? One man can only do so much. If a minister is assuming a responsibility for study and work in political and social activity, how is he going to have the time to do the calling and the praying and the sermon preparation that is necessary if he is to really meet the needs of the people who seek help from the Church? If I come to find my minister in a time of need I don't want to hear that he is away at some meeting on slum clearance.

Exponent: I appreciate your point and I recognize that you raise a real problem. There have been ministers who have been too concerned for general needs of men to meet the particular needs around them, just as there are Christian individuals who are too busy in worthwhile activities to say their prayers. But the two tasks are not entirely separate. I would hope that a minister of a congregation which had in it all sorts and conditions of men would, in his parish calling, in his work of meeting particular problems, be all the while gaining a grasp of what life is really like in that community, and what problems need to be met on a larger scale than just one individual's altruistically meeting specific needs— whether material or spiritual.

Critic: You seem to be assuming that the minister is the only one who can do anything about these things.

Exponent: I may have sounded that way and I wouldn't want to leave that impression for a minute. I'm glad you raised it. As a matter of fact, the main contribution that the minister can make to social reform is to inspire his laymen to take up these responsibilities themselves. He can't personally serve on all the committees that are working in the community, even if the causes are very worthwhile. He can't personally promote all the reforms that should be promoted. But he can hope that the Christian people in his congregation more and more are being inspired to do these things—each man according to his own gifts and according to his own claims on his time. Why? Because the way the minister looks at his whole task and the fact that his total experience, which is tied to his pastoral work and his meeting of particular personal needs, has given him a breadth of understanding which can stimulate the thinking of other people along the same lines and, indeed, the action of other people along the same lines.

Critic: But, isn't there a problem here deeper than just the problem of the minister's time? If, as you say, a minister takes a particular political stand on a particular issue in order to inspire his people to assume their responsibility as citizens, he's very liable to be on the wrong side politically. I may have facts at my disposal that he doesn't have or there may be facts that I consider better than his facts. If I come to church and hear this man, isn't there going to be a block that's going to keep me from coming to church when I have to see a man before me who is taking a political stand that I think is ill-founded?

Exponent: It may be. And what you've said should be a caution to us in the clergy to be as careful and discriminating about the facts as we can and as tentative about those things we're not sure of. But I hope that if we're really preaching the Gospel, the whole Gospel, that all along we've gotten across one very important idea and even our errors may praise God if we've gotten this idea across. Namely, that the people motivated by the best of intentions may nevertheless be wrong, and that all of us should view ourselves critically in the light of our own fallibility. One of the worst things in the world is the dogmatism of people who always think they're right.

Critic: I'm reminded here of a man who was charged by an acquaintance with always claiming to be right. The man grudgingly admitted, "Well, I was once wrong," and the acquaintance asked, "When was that?" The man retorted, "When I admitted that I made a mistake."

Exponent: Well, the Christian Gospel does have a judgment on that sort of thing. I think it important to get people accustomed to expect human fallibility and at the same time to respect sincerity of motive and recognize the importance of reaching better answers to meet the same problems. If that is gotten across, even the mistakes of a minister have been all to the good.

CHAPTER TWO

"Isn't the Church too indefinite about social and political issues, too removed from important concerns?"

CRITIC: In discussing the Church and politics, I was taking the position that the Church shouldn't be getting itself mixed up so much with political and social questions. Some of my friends, I found, however, had a much stronger answer for me than you had. They contended that the Church wasn't in politics enough, that it should be much more involved in real political action, that it should come to grips with the issues. In fact, they said that the Church was still concerned with "pie in the sky bye and bye"; in other words, they charged the Church with just getting individuals to heaven and not caring about the real concerns of people here and now.

Exponent: Certainly we do have to focus primarily on individuals and on getting them set right. I would agree to that much of the charge. But as far as the Church's relationship to the here-and-now is concerned, we take the position that generally the most effective persons for putting the activities of this world on a right basis will be those who have the resources and perspectives which come from being tied to the eternal meaning of things. In other words, we believe that the best way to save society is to save the individuals within it.

Critic: Yes, but isn't this just what ministers always do when they want to play it safe? They confine themselves to the concerns of individuals, and they never go out on a limb as to the real concerns of people in their community life—and thus they offend nobody.

Exponent: Play it safe? Have you noticed who was speaking out as to the abuses of freedom in the Congressional investigative process? Ministers from their pulpits, more than anyone else. Do you see who it is in community after community condemning the evils of segregation? Again, ministers in their pulpits. And these are not uniformly safe positions to take in the particular communities in which these positions are being maintained, either.

Critic: This may be true in certain rare, conspicuous instances, but my friends tell me that there are many other instances where ministers and Church people have dodged the real issues confronting them. They have followed the safe line by just not talking about the things that were the real sources of controversy.

Exponent: In all honesty, I am glad you brought that up. There's no way, of course, of making a statistical check of how many clergy or how many congregations have fulfilled their responsibilities in the name of God to the society in which they live. But we must remember that for every courageous sermon quoted in the newspapers, there have been hundreds of others which have not been quoted, each of which in its own way may well have dealt with one or another aspect of the nature of our common life as God would have us live it. But I agree; sometimes the clergy have followed a safe course and have deliberately kept their heads in the sand—ostrich-like—to avoid seeing what's going on, and all we can say there is that in so doing they do not stand in the great tradition of the Judaeo-Christion heritage.

Critic: Great tradition you say. Isn't this matter of speaking out on issues fairly recent?

Exponent: Recent! What could have been more outspoken than Amos' strictures against the treatment of the poor in Bethel? And you have doubtless heard of the courageous stand of St. Ambrose, Bishop of Milan, who stood at the cathedral steps, barring the entry of the emperor until he would repent the horror of having purged a whole city which met his disfavor. We certainly can't forget Wilberforce, the English Evangelical, who led the crusade for the abolition of slavery in the British Empire.

Critic: But that's all a long time ago, isn't it?

Exponent: Well, more recently when the Churches spoke out against abuses in the Congressional investigation of Communism, it wasn't one pulpit or even one denomination. All of the major non-Roman communions, speaking through the National Council of Churches' General Board, came out with the most trenchant criticism and the most constructive proposal of the lines along which reform should be undertaken.

Critic: If this is the tradition of the Church, why doesn't it do it more heartily and more effectively? For instance, I have never heard of the Church providing its members with a voter's guide that would help them in their voting. And if the Church really feels that political guidance is its task, why doesn't it actually draft legislation and organize its members around it?

Exponent: This is exactly what the Church should not be doing. The Church is not infallible as to the answers in these realms. We have no word from on high that John Jones will make a better senator than Robert Smith.

Critic: Your mention of the name Smith reminds me that in the 1928 Presidential campaign a lot of preachers didn't mind naming names.

Exponent: I'm sorry to say that I do recall that, and frankly, it forms a pretty sorry chapter in the history of this whole business.

Critic: But isn't there ever an occasion when a particular candidate is so evil that the Church should condemn him outright?

Exponent: No, it would never be right for the

Church to condemn the man. But if the meaning of a man's public career has become completely intertwined with an evil position, then the Church needn't be too coy in avoiding the mentioning of a name if it condemns the position.

Critic: I suppose especially if the position has gotten named after the man.

Exponent: Right.

Critic: But wouldn't this naming of names work to encourage candidates to take a stand on issues in Christian terms?

Exponent: Perhaps. But at the same time it would be likely to breed hypocrisy, as the old religious tests for office used to. And further, we would be in for a lot of political machinations within the Church to engineer the endorsement of candidates.

Critic: You mentioned legislation?

Exponent: Yes, there are dangers in backing particular men. I don't see the same objection to churches backing a piece of worthwhile legislation. But we have no divine sanction to say that a particular set of mechanics to achieve a given end would be more effective than another set of mechanics.

Critic: Well, if the minister can't get behind particular people or particular bills, doesn't this mean that he loses his rights as a citizen?

Exponent: Not at all. As a citizen, he certainly can and he should, in so far as he can make up his mind about a given issue or candidate, get into as much action on it as any other citizen could. He can vote as he wishes, he can even make a speech for a candidate, or join a committee for the pushing of certain legislation. But he can't do this in the name of the Church, nor should he from his pulpit.

Critic: What does he say from his pulpit then?

Exponent: Here I get back to my first point. There's the continuing task of trying to bring into individual lives that judgment and grace which will produce more effective personal and social concern on the part of those who hear; but the minister does more than that about social issues. Certainly when laws, conditions, and the behavior of public leaders and citizens are not in accordance with the will of God he has the right and duty to denounce them.

Critic: Now aren't you saying, then, that the minister does not have the right to speak for anything, but only has the right to say what is wrong? Doesn't this leave him with a rather grim and negative task?

Exponent: The two tasks, pointing the right direction and condemning what is wrong, go hand in hand. He tries to hold before people the vision of what the will of God is in particular realms of human relationship, and then he compares with this yardstick what is actually going on. This is the task of prophecy which belongs to the pulpit.

Critic: Prophecy? You mean foretelling what is to come a thousand years from now?

Exponent: That's not primarily what prophecy means. As the old saying goes, prophecy is not fore-telling, it is forth-telling. The prophet, taking his view from the eternal level, being one whose thoughts are focused on God, so looks at the particular present situation in the light of this eternal perspective that he sees the nature of things in a way that is different from those who are earthbound.

Critic: Oh, so you mean that what we always thought was prophecy just isn't so? It doesn't have anything to do with the future at all?

Exponent: It does have, in one sense. If we can get a clear understanding of the meaning of the present in the light of the past and the way God would look at the present situation, we are going to be in a better position to know what the future will be than those who see the whole picture merely from the point of view of the present. In other words, a prophet can say that if a nation continues to live in a way that does violence to the will of God, bringing harm and hurt to great numbers of its citizens—through gross inequalities and lack of oppor-tunity—then that nation is doomed; there will be in-ternal disorder and the nation will be weakened as against the pressures of its enemies. It was in this sense that Amos was able to predict the fall of Samaria. And this, indeed, is a very important task.

Critic: But why is the minister any more gifted in this task than anyone else? What does he have to say to me that I can't find out for myself?

Exponent: Essentially nothing, because each according to the measure of his own ability is supposed to be a minister of God and should be looking at the current scene and his part in it in exactly this way, namely, as much as he can from God's viewpoint. And that's true of the layman as it is of the minister. But the minister, by his very vocational situation, is presumably able to spend more time seeking to know the will of God; presumably he has a more intimate experience of the whole tradition of viewing history and day-to-day life in the light of eternal meanings. It's something like the skill with which the citizens of Oberammergau enact the great Passion Play. They are members of families who all along have taken these roles. It is a bent of mind and makeup that has become characteristic of them as persons. So, too, the minister stands in "the goodly fellowship of the prophets," as we say, part of a continuous outfit who have been engaged in this task and have engaged in study and in prayer to make them more—we'll say—apt instruments of God's judgment on the evils of society. Any society which does not have some men especially dedicated to the task of being watchmen of the Lord will eventually get in a rut. The Biblical proverb tells us that where there is no vision the people perish.

Critic: This is quite true but how can we have enough of such prophets? A minister is only one man and he has many other things to do, including his whole ministry to individuals that you mentioned earlier, as well as his life of study and prayer which, after all, makes his prophecy possible. There are so many problems of such a complex nature in our communities and our common life that I think it's beyond the scope of any one minister or any group of ministers to deal with them. Where are they going to get the time to do all the things that they're called upon to do in their ministry to individuals as well as their prophetic function?

Exponent: This brings us right back to where we were at the end of the last session and I hope that it represents a special challenge to laymen. The clergy can speak out on particularly grave issues or even personally engage in group action in regard to particularly critical situations in a given community. But the great hope is that this very activity which becomes characteristic of his life will be contagious, and that for every minister there will be fifty to a hundred laymen who are, each in his own way, covering some aspect of the front. If the Church people of America were to join the ministry in this task of witnessing to the society around us in terms of God's will for it, there would certainly be a change in things, even in the most depressing community situations. The most organized and long-continued evils would go down before it.

Critic: That all sounds very good, but a good many secular people say that the Church doesn't do this kind of thing rapidly enough. For instance, one of my friends left the Church because he couldn't wait for it. He was very much concerned with social problems and he felt that the Church was so slow that he had to leave it and express his concern in secular social-action groups.

Exponent: The question isn't one of *either/or*; it's one of *both/and*. We've got to remember that even the most secular minded social-action groups have in the long run received their principles and inspiration from the Judaeo-Christian heritage. And, too, we are hoping that laymen will express in specific terms in society what the Church has inspired them to do by getting into particular groups which will be free to endorse particular candidates and press for particular legislation— which the Church is not free to do.

Critic: I see what you mean by *both/and* rather than *either/or*, but I wonder if the Church has really made this connection clear.

Exponent: I think the Church has made clear enough the responsibility of the citizen to vote and to take seriously his civic responsibility, but I would concede the Church needs to do a lot more—to encourage the Christian laymen to bring to bear a critical view of the *status quo* and, for that matter, a critical view of the proposed reforms in the light of the eternal principles of our religion.

Critic: But doesn't the Church have to be careful that this doesn't become just a matter of *words*? Isn't it true that part of the Christian message is that these eternal principles must be expressed through some kind of real involvement in the particular concerns of men?

Exponent: That's right. In fact, that is a necessary follow-up of the Christian belief in the Incarnation. At the center of our religion is the affirmation that God Himself entered our earthly estate and became involved in our life.

Critic: I think I can see more clearly the relationship of the Church to political, social, and economic issues, but why is it that so many laymen in the Church protest against this very thing?

Exponent: Well, there are a number of reasons. One I think is a plain misunderstanding on their part, and sometimes it's a misunderstanding on the part of ministers themselves. It's not an easy thing to get clear in our minds how to avoid a direct political promotion in the name of the Church on the one hand, and the thing we know we don't want on the other hand, to avoid indifference to the corporate concerns of men. But you've already suggested another reason for what we sometimes meet in churches taking a position. Some ministers have been silent so long on matters of this sort that the people have come to think that the silent treatment is the normal way for the Church. Well, actually the surprise shown in recent months that certain prominent ministers had been tied into so many social reform movements, and the feeling that this in itself was the wrong thing and must indicate some kind of subversion, is a reflection on the fact that not enough ministers have been tied into enough movements. Those particular people who were out in the forefront shouldn't have appeared in the forefront so much. There should have been such a goodly company surrounding them that it would have been preposterous to call it subversion to have been concerned for social reform.

But I think it has to be admitted too that certain parts of the Church have in particular times in past history, and even in recent decades, acted wrongly in this regard. Actually backing particular legislation has not worked out too well and this has disillusioned people about this particular role of the Church. And sometimes the Church has been too active against particular candidates. You've already mentioned an embarrassing instance in that regard. But there is a deeper reason, I think, and we should explore that for a moment.

There are some laymen who wouldn't complain for a minute if the Church came out on a public question as long as the Church was on the side of the *status quo*— on the side that protects or backs up their own personal or group interest. It is when the Church asks for a change in the *status quo* or questions it—particularly where this change would affect the interests of these laymen—that they get very interested in this question of the Church in politics.

Critic: Well, that's true, isn't it? What they are protesting against is not the Church in politics but the Church in politics that they don't agree with.

Exponent: That's right. There's no American churchman, no matter how conservative his stand, who criticizes Bishop Dibelius for his forthright opposition to Communist oppression in East Germany.

Critic: That's because practically everybody is opposed to Communism.

Exponent: But not in East Germany—and certainly the Government there isn't. But in any case the Church cannot govern its positions by following majorities. The Church has often taken very unpopular positions.

Critic: Yes but we have to make a distinction, don't we? All churchmen would agree that the Church has to oppose Communism because it's atheistic. After all the Communists come right out and say that they don't believe in God. But the situation is different where political and social questions are involved.

Exponent: Well, there is a great difference of degree in Communism. But I don't think I can accept your distinction that Communism doesn't represent political and social questions. Communism is a political and social question, but like all political and social questions, fundamental religious issues are at stake. But that's actually the case when other public questions are involved. I think we have got to remember that God is not interested only in His good name; that is, that atheism is not the only evil in the world. Slums, denial of freedom, segregation, inequality of opportunity, all these things look just like social questions or political questions, but they, too, all stem from deep religious and ethical perversions. The reason why people tolerate these things or even endorse them is that they have gotten their ethics or even their theology mixed up, and the Church can't be silent about any of these things.

Critic: I agree. As a matter of fact, silence as much as speech implies a certain political attitude. Either by default or action the Church is in politics.

Exponent: That's just the point. And it's much better for the Church openly to recognize the role it has to play in this regard, one way or another, and thus be self-critical about the way it plays it, rather than simply being for something because it has not taken thought as to which side it ought to be on. The layman especially, whose mind naturally is taken up with many day-to-day concerns, has to be reminded over and over again that when he doesn't take a concern, when he doesn't react toward a public question, he is in effect casting a vote for the *status quo.* If this is what his religious and ethical principles call for that is fine but we don't want it to be a matter of simply doing so by default. God is interested in all that concerns the welfare of man, and the Church should be interested in no less. As the Prophet Amos said in justifying his preaching on social questions, "The Lord God has spoken: who can but prophesy."

CHAPTER THREE

"Does Communism provide a better dynamic for social change than Christianity?"

CRITIC: We have been discussing the various ways in which the Church concerns itself with social and political concerns. This is all very good and I think I understand now that the Church ought to be concerned in these matters and is doing a creditable job in studying them and talking about them. I wonder sometimes if talking, however, is enough. The Communists say that this is just what the Church always does. It merely talks about social reform and social betterment, and never gets beyond that. What kind of an answer can I have for these Communists who say that the Church doesn't provide any real action in these areas? They say that Communism provides a better dynamic for social improvement and change than Christianity.

Exponent: I'm glad you raised this, knowing that you are no Communist and that you are eager to get before us the answer to what has been a common charge ever since the rise of the Communist movement. I'll admit that in theory it would seem that if a group of people mean business about social change they ought to organize and bring it about. And I know that much of the appeal of Communism, particularly in countries where social conditions have been especially deplorable, has been its bold promise to get at these conditions immediately and effect a change.

Critic: Yes, that's just the point. These people say the Communists can go into action immediately, whereas the Church is painfully long-range in its approach.

Exponent: The Church is long-range about many things. By the very nature of our understanding of the universe and man's destiny, we take the long view because we believe that every individual has eternal life. God has a lot of time to work these things out.

Critic: Yes, but these people charge the Church with talking about heaven, when the real needs of people are for bread right here and now. Doesn't this talk about rewards hereafter and all that serve to confirm the charge that Lenin made that religion is merely some kind of opiate for the people?

Exponent: I confess that there have been times in Christian history in some parts of the world where something like this has been very much the case, when the Church has served as a buttress to evil conditions and used its emphasis upon the life to come as a way of sort of numbing people to putting up with bad conditions now.

Critic: An example of that, I suppose, would be the

connection between the old Russian Orthodox Church and the Tsar's regime. Perhaps this accounts for the particular fury of the Soviet State against Christianity in Russia.

Exponent: I think it does in part account for it. But that doesn't completely explain it. The Marxist system and the Christian thought about the destiny of man are radically different. There is no real reconciliation possible even if the Church had not been so much tied up with a tyrannous state there. But I concede that at times the Church has used its other-worldly emphasis as a device to support evil conditions. There is no way of denying that. But that is not the genuine Christian tradition.

Critic: Well, then, what would you say is the genuine Christian tradition on this?

Exponent: We should look at the Old and New Testament and the history of the Church since, and we see all through a concern with conditions here and now, though we do not confine man's destiny to threescore and ten years. That means that we can *now* promote the best way to remedy things, even when the best way seems to involve a slower process.

Critic: But under this kind of system there will be many people who will die without ever seeing things righted.

Exponent: Unfortunately, yes. We believe in eternal life for the individual; so while we do earnestly strive to get things righted as soon as they can be—taking into account all the factors and trying to avoid doing more harm while we achieve good—yet all the while we do know that even a person who had a hard lot and can never enjoy what would be the will of God for his life in this world, still has all eternity ahead of him, where we can presume things will be better for those who are on God's side.

Critic: This is all very interesting. But it doesn't answer the concern of a person who seems to need food today more than eternal bliss in some distant future.

Exponent: I agree that we can never for a minute be distracted from attention to pressing problems now. My only point is that if the best way to work out a change and to preserve everybody's integrity takes a little longer, we feel a little freer about letting a little longer time pass than do those who feel that life is over in three-score and ten years. One point I haven't brought out yet that bears on this part of our discussion is the fact that sudden social change forced from above often destroys as much as it creates, violating human personality and leaving no room for free human decision. The Utopian schemes of the Communists generally involve reducing the individual to simply a unit in the scheme or a pawn on the chessboard. Now the Judaeo-Christian heritage has always been concerned that there be room for individual differences and free decision as to the exercise of differing talents and interests. This, too, is a value on this earth no less than in the life to come.

Critic: But won't the real freedom of the individual evolve after these practical economic matters are straightened out? It is said by the Communists that the resulting peace would allow the individual human personality to flower in a new and better way.

Exponent: Well, that criticism, which I appreciate is not your own but simply aimed to bring before us what the Communist line is on this point, overlooks completely a dimension of Christian thinking which is a safeguard against a dreamy Utopianism. If people were always nice to each other when they had plenty of money or plenty of food, then we could perhaps reason that when everybody had plenty, then there would be perfect peace and freedom for every individual. But we have had too many examples in a free enterprise society that individuals who are well fed are not necessarily agreeable. Not only that, to achieve these sudden reforms necessarily implies a leadership of tyranny.

Critic: Yes, but the Communists say that this tyranny is not really tyranny, it is simply the necessary control by leaders whose intentions are good.

Exponent: I'd be willing to concede that some Communist leaders may have had good intentions at the start. But human history shows, and this is very basic to the Christian understanding of man, that when absolute power is in the hands of anyone it almost inevitably corrupts him, and that tyranny seems an inevitable result from the cencentration of power. I think we have had sufficient examples from the recent history of Communism to show that this has almost inevitably been so in terms of the abuse of human beings. I refer to purges, and the manifest cruelty, and so forth.

Critic: The Communist himself, I think, would agree with you that this is the case during the early transitional period, the phase they sometimes called the dictatorship of the proletariat. But this is taken, however, to be a temporary expedient.

Exponent: Yes, I know—until the great day comes in, and then we won't need any government at all. But this overlooks the strong tendency of people to hold on to control once they have it, and the inevitability of strong controls in a socialist state. When things are being run from the center, there have to be strong controls, and with those controls come corruption and tyranny and callousness toward individual fulfillment. This really is an expression of Original Sin.

Critic: Original Sin? You mean the Garden of Eden and all that?

Exponent: Well, the Adam and Eve narrative does tell us a lot about ourselves. We are capable on the one hand of being well-meaning; we yearn to serve God and our fellow-men; but at the same time there is a strong self-centering tendency which is at the root of all our particular sins ——

Critic: But what's that got to do with the subject?

Exponent: It means that no individual can be trusted with too much power. This isn't only because more power increases the damage an evil man can do; but also the possession of power itself operates as a cause of self-centeredness and helps blind a man to his own weaknesses, to his own fallibilities. As Lord Acton has so well said, and I had this statement in mind in my earlier comments, "Power corrupts; absolute power corrupts absolutely."

Critic: Now are you implying that democracy takes account of Original Sin more than Communism does?

Exponent: It certainly does. Hence the careful system of checks and balances in our Constitution and our doctrine of separation of powers.

Critic: I think I can agree with you that a religiously grounded democracy, with its precautions against tyranny and its protections for the individual, is in the long run a better dynamic for sound social change. But we must realize that in America we have been blessed with great natural resources and, judged by other countries, our people are well-fed and well-housed. Isn't the situation perhaps somewhat different in lands where people are threatened with actual starvation?

Exponent: The last thing I would want to be put on record as saying is that I'm not concerned about the starving millions or that we don't want better living conditions for people even in terms of material benefits.

We do want this. But I must assert again, in the name of the Church, that man cannot live by bread alone. Having a house and food is not the only thing man wants, and if he must achieve some degree of material well-being at the cost of freedom of thought and freedom of expression, freedom to be an individual, I think it is too high a price to pay. I can say this somewhat because I'm not convinced that in the long run even man's *material* well-being is furthered by an authoritarian society. Don't you think that most of the great improvements, inventions and scientific progress which have made man's lot on earth easier have come from the impetus of individual effort, and, I must say, individual effort stimulated by the profit motive?

Critic: Well, now, I wonder if the profit motive is so Christian a thing. Isn't this profit motive based on selfishness and greed?

Exponent: In a measure it is; but Christianity, as I have said, is a realistic faith and it deals with men as they are. I grant that people ought to strive as hard as they can to benefit their fellow men entirely from altruistic aims, and Christianity has stimulated this kind of effort all through its history. But the fact is that we are living after the fall of man, theologically speaking. In other words, self-centeredness and self-interest are primary factors in man's existence. Where Christianity is a great deal more realistic than Communism or other Utopian schemes is in its recognition of the actual makeup of

man, which makes it inevitable that the immediate appli-
cation of a Utopia is doomed because men are as they
are. That's why the Church must always make it its first
concern to redeem individuals and why the Church
must be opposed to schemes which overlook the nature
of sinful man and which, almost inevitably then, involve
the prospects of tyranny and destructiveness, and thus
reduce the possibilities of man's coming out of his selfishness and self-interest.

Critic: But isn't this all rather subtle and sophisticated? People who have traveled behind the Iron Curtain
very often state that Communism seems to provide a
dynamic appeal for young people that Western Christian civilization doesn't. Young people want to see things
happen right now.

Exponent: Yes, that is a tendency of youth (and, by
the way, I think it is one reason why we must be very
chary of branding people as Communists or dangerous
citizens because in high school or college they may have,
in their youthful zeal, belonged to some organization or
other that turned out to be Communist-dominated). But
in terms of an ideal for society, we have to think of
things in mature terms, indeed—if you wish to use your
word—in sophisticated terms. I personally believe that
Christianity, when presented as a religion of action, is
certainly capable of arousing the response of youth. On
the other hand, youth can become rather easily disillusioned with a movement like Communism, as we can

note from the large number of young people who have sought to get from East Germany into West Germany recently.

Critic: As a matter of fact, I heard the story recently of members of East German Christian youth groups who made a public witness of their faith in the face of demands that they renounce it. This happened in school rooms where, in the guise of public tests, rejection of Christianity was being pressured.

Exponent: That's very inspiring. But in any case, the question is not what appeals to youth. A lot of youth were attracted by Hitler and the Nazis. The question is what, in the mature judgment of the centuries, we find happens to people when social change is brought about by blackjack methods rather than by the free persuasion of the people affected.

Critic: Now this gets us back to something that we've been talking about a great deal, and that is the importance of the protection of the individual as a Christian virtue. Couldn't it be said that there are other virtues that are equally Christian, such as the virtue of equality? And it may well be that the Communists might be right in asserting that they carry out the will of God better by achieving equality for people than the Christians who hold so firmly to the values of individuality at the expense of equality.

Exponent: First of all, I don't think the Communists have done so well in achieving equality. As a matter of fact, old-time theoretical Marxists regret these days that Communism as it actually expresses itself in the Soviet orbit is a far cry from the ideal of equality. There are gradations of income; gradations of advantages; gradations of housing; and of rank; and now, of uniform. But even taking Communism on a theoretical basis, equality is not a simple ideal. I think what we mean, if we are going to give proper recognition to individual differences and individual self-fulfillment, is equality of opportunity: in other words, an equal chance for everyone to develop his particular gifts and skills.

Critic: Then you're saying that Christianity stands for both equality and individuality, which means we can't be for a simple equality?

Exponent: That's right. That fits it, I think.

Critic: But here again the Communist has an argument against you. He would say that his system provides better for the development of skills and talents in the whole population of society. His charge would be that in a Western society, education becomes limited to the sons and daughters of those classes in society that have the benefit of the means to send their sons and daughters to favored schools and colleges.

Exponent: That comment is unrealistic. It doesn't take into account the degree to which education on all levels is available to all sorts and conditions of men— though I agree we have a long way to go in America to fulfill our own ideal in this regard. Let's go back to the kind of education that's involved in a state in which there is authoritarian rule. If this education is conducted under a fear of freedom of expression and a constraint on freedom of research, then there's a qualitative factor here that we've got to look to even if you could show me that quantitatively behind the Iron Curtain they had extended education benefits further than we have, which I doubt very much. Now as between an educational pattern in which there is not yet full equality of opportunity, but where there is a free atmosphere for an individual to express himself, and one in which there is more possibility of attending school, but a restraint upon the expression of the faculty, I would take the former.

Critic: So, here again, then, you come back to freedom as the critical difference between Communism and a Western Christian social point of view. Isn't this just the issue? Communists will argue with you that you can never have true freedom unless you have security. Without security, they would say, there simply isn't the kind of choice available to the individual which gives the word "freedom" any real content or meaning.

Exponent: Well, now, security is important and I want to stress again that the basic securities of individuals, the basic supplies that keep life going—food, clothes, shelter—are a concern of Western Christian civilization and a concern of the Church. Security is important for its own sake, that the sons of God may be happy people and not live in fear. But security is also important for the sake of freedom; I agree with you there, too. But in our society we've been increasing the security of people and at the same time we've been preserving their freedom in the process. Now when it comes to a conflict of freedom and security—and I think that is basically the conflict between our social order in its present stage and Communism in any form—I will certainly stand on the side of freedom without security rather than the side of security without freedom. And I feel that's God's side, too. I think we've got to go back and understand the basic Christian doctrine of Creation here. When God gave us freedom He took a great risk. He could have run us as marionettes. He could have had a perfect society. He'd have simply pulled the strings and we would have behaved toward each other the way we ought to. But He took the risk of giving us freedom, which means we're free to behave rather badly toward each other, we're free to disorganize things badly. He starts, as Genesis tells us, with the grand task of reducing chaos to order and we're supposed to help Him do it; but we can reduce order to chaos just about as fast as He can put things in order again. That's the risk He took with our freedom and I think that we can't reverse that if we understand the whole nature of man, the whole nature of creation. Since God took the risk that man may not always have security, we then have to take that risk and give men freedom even at the risk of the loss of their security or a slower developing security.

You can see why it is that the Communists have been against Christianity, entirely apart from the failings of Christianity in the past, in countries where the Communists have taken over, the failings that you and I would grant. They really cannot suffer to exist by their side a system that has a view of man and his destiny which makes so much of freedom and of the individual. They can't stand to have side by side with them a system which does see eternity as part of the dimension of man's life. Now, men who really hold and understand the Christian faith will only yield to an authoritarian society when they're forced to, whereas if that faith can be destroyed in people, then people will more readily yield to the fatuous Utopianism which Marxism represents. And that's why in the long run the best defense against Communism is the deepening and the extension of a vital Christian faith.

CHAPTER FOUR

"Is the Church tinged with Communism?"

CRITIC: Having arrived at the conclusion that there were certain irreconcilable oppositions between the Christian Gospel and Communism I now have another question about this. Isn't it somewhat strange that although the Church itself claims this opposition between the Christian Gospel and Communism, it is charged by so many people with being tinged with Communism? If there is this opposition, why is it that the Church repeatedly opens itself up to this charge of being Communist and the clergy of the Church open themselves to the charge of being influenced by or related to the Communist movement?

Exponent: You are right to stress that there is an irreconcilable conflict between the Christian faith and Communism; and as a matter of fact, the best defense against the spread of Communistic ideas is the clear exposition of the Christian Gospel. But as to the Churches being "tinged with Communism," I know the charges you mean; I have been reading the papers and magazines too. But do you really believe that there has been proof that there are actual Communists among the ministry of the Church?

Critic: Well, I wouldn't want to say that there has been actual proof that ministers have been active Communists, but it is a fact that various ministers have been mentioned by the investigators as being Communists or being subversive in that they choose to say the same things and support the same causes that the Communists do. One would think that where there is this much smoke there might be some fire.

Exponent: Though there has been a great shortage of proof along these lines, I would not be inclined to disagree with you that there may have been some ministers who have been pretty consciously fellow-traveling with the Communist cause, but I feel that the number has been greatly exaggerated.

Critic: Didn't a former investigator for one of the Congressional committees, in a very careful study, state that there were over seven thousand Communists among the Protestant clergy?

Exponent: Obviously neither you nor I are acquainted with the full record of every minister named in the article to which you refer, but you and I do know something about our own Church, and I want to say that if that article was as grossly inaccurate as to other Churches as it was to the Episcopal Church, we can't take the figure of seven thousand seriously at all.

Critic: Didn't he head this list of prominent Communist collaborators with the names of at least eight Episcopal bishops?

Exponent: That he did. And this gives a pretty good example of the research methods which must have been used. Out of the people he calls "top leaders" in the churches, three of these bishops have been retired for years and are so labeled, one of them is not the bishop of the diocese named and is retired though not so labeled. Now that leaves us four retired bishops and, with all due respect to retired bishops, they are not top leaders in the forefront of the clergy. And again, one of the other bishops, and this is very surprising indeed, is not only long dead but his successor in office is dead. I refer to the Bishop of Atlanta, two bishops ago, who was listed as a present, active top collaborator. And one of the bishops named appeared to be fictional, one "William David Short."

Critic: Maybe he just got the name of the diocese wrong.

Exponent: No, it's worse than that. A careful check shows that there never was a bishop with such a name in the whole history of our Church and, in fact, in the whole of the Anglican Communion throughout the world.

Critic: As I've been following you, that leaves two bishops out of his eight, and still might be serious.

Exponent: But I think I've proved my point which is that the numbers have been exaggerated. Now as for these two bishops, both of them are bishops of small dioceses, in no case top leaders of the Christian cause. Both of them are very fine men doing a good job where they are, and, in fact, neither of them could remotely be called a Communist in any sense of the word. My point is that if this is a sample of the kind of research which has gone into these large claims of Communist infiltration of the Churches, we really can't take these claims very seriously. And this question of checking up on the names of people who hold official position in Churches isn't so difficult, you know. After all, we have the *Episcopal Church Annual*.

Critic: Well, granted that there may be some deficiencies in the research methods of these investigators and that the numbers of subversives in the Church may be, in fact, exaggerated, aren't revelations of this sort still a good thing if it means that the very few subversives that are real subversives are uncovered? Doesn't this alert the public to still another threat that Communism presents?

Exponent: It may do that but it does so at a very heavy price. First of all, taking seriously these wholesale claims represents an exact reversal of our American principle that men are presumed to be innocent until proven guilty. But more serious than that is the possible effect on people's attitudes towards the churches. Anything that weakens the confidence of the American public in our churches—our churches which furnish the moral and spiritual resources against Communism—ultimately plays into Communist hands.

Now, I'd like to try out on you an argument so often

used by these people making charges against the churches; namely, that if you happen to have the same object on a given issue at the moment that the Communists do, you must be a Communist. Well, it actually happens that one of the top Communist aims is the weakening of the life of the churches, the breaking down of their morale, and more than that, the weakening of the confidence of the people in the churches. That means you can say that people making these ridiculous wholesale charges, people who are thereby weakening the confidence of American people in their churches, are engaged in Communist collaboration in their very effort to destroy people's loyalty to the Christian Church. Now, just a minute, I don't say that I agree with this approach they themselves use, that if you happen to have the same objects in common that makes you a Communist. But if you use their principle and apply it to this field, you'll find that in their trying to weaken the people in their churches ——

Critic: But you wouldn't, in your concern to protect the moral and spiritual leadership of the Church in this country, want to provide a cloak for the minister who might really be guilty of some subversion, would you?

Exponent: No, not at all. The Church itself should be concerned in disciplining or removing any clergy who are in fact guilty of treason or subversion.

Critic: Do you mean to say that the Government

should have no authority to do anything about a sub-versive planted in the Church by the Communists?

Exponent: I don't mean that, else I'd be claiming some form of "benefit of clergy" out of the Middle Ages. I was simply saying that the Church itself should be concerned. But more than that, the Government itself should have every right to proceed against a min-ister in the same way it would proceed against anyone else, and when I say "in the same way" I mean this: if there is evidence warranting his indictment, his trial and his conviction, these matters should proceed in due order.

Critic: But isn't it true that the greatest danger really comes from those ministers who give their support and lend their prestige to some of the same objectives as the Communists support and promote? For instance, the campaigns for the establishment and promotion of peace, where ministers are very often, it seems to me, guilty of falling into the Communist trap of crying "Peace! Peace!" when there is no peace.

Exponent: I don't happen to be a pacifist but pacifism has always been regarded as a legitimate position which the clergy may hold.

Critic: Yes, I know that, but aren't we planning to discuss that later on?

Exponent: Yes, and when we do get to it I think you'll at least see some of the reasons why some Christian ministers have taken a pacifist position. Now, you'll remember that when the Communists had an alliance with Hitler, the Communists were for a pacifist line so far as this country was concerned, and later, when they broke with Hitler, they took a strongly interventionist position in this country. So obviously, the pacifists sound good to them when they don't want war and the pacifists sound evil to the Communists when the Communists want war. But this doesn't mean that the pacifist is tying up with them either time. He still holds the line that he has been holding, namely, that he doesn't like war under any circumstances. Now, my point is, that there is no guilt simply by what happens to be, for a particular period of time, a mutual objective.

Critic: Yes, but weren't there a good many clergy that protested the execution of the two people who seemed obviously guilty of treason, the Rosenbergs?

Exponent: That furnishes a very good case in point. Let's get off the clergy for a moment and picture this situation. Suppose you are opposed to capital punishment under any and all circumstances. Actually there are some very intelligent people who take that position, so I am not slandering you—and it is not my own position either, I might say. Suppose that another fellow is a relative of the Rosenbergs and has always had an affection for them. Now suppose I am a Communist. Now it may so happen, for the reasons that I have just stated, that all three of us are opposed to the execution of the Rosenbergs. You, because you don't want anybody executed, no matter what he has done; this other fellow because he likes the Rosenbergs; and I don't want them executed because, we'll say, I am a Communist. Now we may all be wrong and I am quite sure we all would be, but that proves nothing whatsoever about your being a Communist and it proves nothing whatsoever about this other fellow's being a Communist just because maybe I am. What I am trying to say is that we cannot establish guilt by mutual object. Quite frankly there are a lot of things the Communists want that I want. The Communist likes to be comfortably housed and well-fed. I like those things myself, but that doesn't make me a Communist. More than that, if I would like people as a whole to be well-housed, that doesn't prove me a Communist just because Communists have purported to want that for people.

Critic: Well, I can see your point there, but what really disturbs me more than just the accidental sharing of objectives between Communists and church people is the fact that a great many ministers have allowed their names to appear on letterheads of organizations that are definitely subversive and in many cases have often worked hand in glove with these people.

Exponent: Yes, I know that has happened. It's a pretty complicated subject though, because there are such a variety of situations.

Critic: I don't think it is so complicated. It seems very clear to me that it implies one of two things: that these people who let their names appear on this kind of material are either sympathetic to the Communist aims or they are "dupes."

Exponent: It could imply either of those two things, but I think generally it has not. Often an organization is set up for a perfectly legitimate aim—one that might commend itself to you or me—and a minister is brought into the picture because of the fact that names of people he trusts are associated with the organization, though he may not know anything at all about some on the list. Now some of these unknown names may turn out to have subversive connections or—as has been the case over and over—people with subversive connections have often muscled into these organizations, and because they are often more active than those who are patriotic and loyal, they end up dominating the purposes and directions of the outfit.

Critic: Isn't it very careless of a minister, then, to let himself be used by an organization which has in it people whose real aims and objectives are totally unknown to him?

Exponent: It can be careless or, on the other hand, if we set as stringent a standard as you have implied, it would mean nobody could join anything because there are few people in the country who are so well acquainted with every possible person who might appear on a long organization list for a new association that he would be able to spot the exact motives and the exact connections of everyone. But I think it is worth saying that anybody who would take the responsibility of going on the board of an organization or letting his name be used has to keep in pretty close touch with its meetings and its issuances so that he will be alerted as to the situation and thus will know if he ought to withdraw. I grant that with all the preoccupations of a minister, sometimes this duty has not been sufficiently attended to.

Critic: Isn't there a simple solution for this? He just has to stay out of such things entirely.

Exponent: This comment would apply to all citizens, I suppose; and let's see where it leads. It was DeToqueville, I believe, who commented that one of the most wholesome things about American democracy was the fact that a good deal of the work of social progress and social altruism has been done in this country by voluntary groups, which means you don't have to have a strong government on the one hand nor do you end up with simple anarchy or failure to get things done on the other. Now this principle of—well—we can call it "voluntary associationism," has been an important part of our life. If we end up saying that nobody dare join any group for any purpose for fear that somebody might end up in the picture who would give a bad repute to the organization, then I think a very important part of the very structure and dynamics of our American life will have collapsed. I say this with some feeling—and with a bad conscience I might say—because nowadays I throw most appeals for any purpose in the basket simply because I haven't time to run a check on all the people who are listed. And I am sure that in doing that, I do a great injustice time and time again, and am failing to do my part in the support of worthwhile causes. And I might add that it's a pretty neat rationalization to avoid signing a check and giving sacrificially to a good cause if you can just say, "Well, there might be some Communists in it," or "I don't know who these people are."

Critic: That may well be—when the object is obviously good; but what about the case of organizations whose object is obviously in favor of the international Communist movement such as these councils for Soviet-American friendship? What justification was there for so many ministers joining these organizations, as many of them did?

Exponent: Speaking in general terms I wouldn't say the aim is obviously wrong. I suppose you have heard of our Lord's injunction to love your enemies! So that, just speaking theoretically now, Soviet friendship doesn't automatically imply a wrong thing. But, I'm not going to take my stand on that in the face of the actual fact that Soviet friendship groups arose at a time when Soviet friendship was a patriotic duty. Now, I agree, being more realistic than I was in first answering you, that Soviet friendship is neither a patriotic duty, nor a safe or tenable position even in realistic Christian terms; but the point is that you and a lot of other people, I'm afraid, have not been sufficiently historically minded. Because Russia is an enemy now, these people forget that there was a time when the Russians were holding the Eastern Front and we were doing all we could to further good relations with them—wisely or not is not the point. Now at the moment we're trying to have very good relations with Franco and Spain. We certainly can't approve of all that goes on there, particularly the religious intolerance, but right now the proper thing to do is to be friendly there because we seem to think it's in our national interest. And I want to add another thought. People forget that many of our most distinguished citizens were involved in those Soviet friendship efforts at that time.

Critic: If this is true, it's most unfortunate that it hasn't been more widely brought out.

Exponent: The fact that it hasn't points to a very sinister thing. A man's connection with, say, a Soviet friendship dinner back in 1944 is usually used against a man that is not liked for some other reason. There has been a tendency in our country for a long time that when people are against a particular bit of legislation or social reform, particularly one that would hurt their own interests, they attach the label "Communist" to it. Such a label can be reinforced if they can drag something out of the past, when the situation was utterly different, which in the popular mind would look like Communist subversion.

Critic: Well, I suppose ministers are particularly subject to this, because they do seem to be engaged, for some reason or other, in a rather constant criticism of society and of the way things are in this country.

Exponent: I think actually you flatter the ministry. I am not sure that throughout the Church we are sufficiently concerned for taking a critical look at things and I'm not sure we're sufficiently concerned in making efforts to improve things along the line of the will of God. But nevertheless, what you say has been the Church at its best. I don't mean the Church has always been right in every position it has taken. We have sufficiently covered that, I think. But the Church is meant to be a leaven within society, seeking to redeem it. It stands over and above any current pattern, mores, or legislation. In fact, I am very much concerned that through fear of charges of guilt by association or guilt by mutual object (that we've already discussed), and through fear of the exaggerated claims of Communist affiliation, the voice of prophecy may be stilled in many quarters; and this would be a loss—not only to the Church's mission, but a loss to our country. Our country has always profited from those who were dedicated to the Kingdom of God and who were seeking to bring this land more in line with the claims of the Kingdom. A kind of false notion has grown up recently that the best patriot is one who says "my country, right or wrong." In the long run, the best patriot is a man who stands with an allegiance even higher than his country and looks critically at his country so that his country may be a better reflection of the heavenly country.

Critic: Yes, I guess that is why a lot of lay people, when they hear ministers engaging in this prophetic function, involving criticism of things as they are very often, feel that the leadership of the churches tends to be sort of radical.

Exponent: That's an interesting word; I think we ought to pause and consider it. In one sense, the Church has to be radical—if we take "radical" in its natural, etymological sense as meaning "going to the root of things." Now the one institution on which we should surely rely for an impartial and objective critique of things, for loyalty to the eternal principles of God, and for going right down to the root of things rather than looking at the surface, is the Church. Men right within the Church can reasonably differ about these things. But the important thing is that the Church can never be content with the *status quo* simply because it is the *status quo.*

Critic: I think I begin to see your point on this. Actually, however, there is a great difference between a Marxist promoting certain social ideas or ideas of social reform and the Church militating for certain ideas that it holds to be necessary to the upbuilding of the Kingdom of God in any society. It's important, however, for our lay people and the ministers in the churches to realize that the radical protest of the Church stems from this ancient prophetic tradition in our Faith that you've been talking about, and therefore it constitutes a healthy radical criticism of society, and that this makes for freedom. But what they should do, it seems to me, is to make it very clear that whereas the Marxist criticism is also a radical criticism, its distortion of the facts of human nature make for tyranny.

Exponent: That's the precise point. I believe the Churches have to devote a good deal of their educational program to an understanding of the theology, if I may call it that, of Communism—an understanding of its errors; and right beside it, point by point, to an understanding of the Christian theology underlying our social concern. And in the long run, as we both agreed before, this is the best defense a nation can have against the threat of Communism, without or within.

CHAPTER FIVE

"Has the Church any business opposing established patterns of segregation?"

CRITIC: When I was growing up there was an established custom that seemed to work quite well. White people went to "white churches" and colored people went to "colored churches," and there wasn't any great problem connected with it. Lately, however, I've noticed that the churches seem to be interfering with this established pattern. A number of churches seem to be demanding that this pattern be broken down, and that people of all backgrounds and races go to all churches. Do you think this is the Church's business, to interfere in these established patterns that have worked so well? Especially since the Church seems to want to change not only its own patterns, but the patterns in the community.

Exponent: I think you've assessed the trend quite correctly. No major Christian group today is content at all with segregation in the life of the Church or in the life of the community. One thing that is expected of us is that we will treat people fairly whoever they are, whatever their background.

Critic: I hold with that just as strongly as you do. I don't believe in treating any human being with any lack of consideration or essential decency. I don't believe in this kind of "second-class citizenship" that one hears about occasionally. This doesn't mean, however, that people cannot be separated. One can arrange separate patterns of life, and yet carry them out with equality of opportunity and decency.

Exponent: That sounds very commendable, but let's just think what it means. Suppose the synod or presbytery or diocese of a Church builds two mission churches in contiguous areas, one for colored people and one for white people. Let's assume that both of them are fitted out with equal good taste, that they are drawn according to identical plans, and that the salaries of their clergy are identical. Yet the fact that we say to a Negro—and, realistically, he is the one we are saying it to—that he is not fit to come in and worship along with us in the white church is, in effect, to treat him as a second-class person. While this is true in the community as well, as regards transportation and schools, hotels and restaurants, the Church must set a higher standard for itself than it can hope to achieve within the same given time within the community as a whole.

Critic: There is a point in what you say regarding the Church's life within itself; but after all, the Church represents only a fraction of the life that we live and is somewhat apart from our established family and community relationships. In fact, there are other occasions upon which non-segregation would seem to be all right, such as a patriotic rally, or ——

Exponent: No, No! You've been convinced too easily. I'm afraid at bottom is a misunderstanding of what the life of the Church should be. I'm afraid sometimes that's the impression that the Church has given, that it represents a very occasional and special and superficial aspect of human relationships—but if the Church *is* the Church, if the Church is the body of Christ as we talk about it in the New Testament, it should be the place where relations are the warmest and firmest, and where the basis of fellowship is the deepest.

Critic: But this is just what I am worried about. This warm fellowship that you are talking about—doesn't this mean that there's going to be the threat of intermarriage?

Exponent: Now you raise a very difficult question, simply because the segregated community is a reality in most parts of the country, in one form or another. It is true that if a young couple comes to me pastorally, asking my counsel on intermarriage where a white person and a colored person are involved, I would have to counsel on two levels; on one level I would have to help the couple recognize the actual burdens which obviously they would have to bear, and perhaps the children would have to bear, regardless of the right or wrong of the situation. And one would have to be very sure that there were sufficient spiritual resources and a deep basis of union, entirely apart from some negative protest, or from the support of some abstract cause, which could sustain them through the pressures that are bound to come from the very first minute of marriage.

Critic: Well, now, that makes sense. I can go along with you on your discouragement of such a marriage.

Exponent: Not so quickly. Let me finish. I would have to assert, and equally firmly, that the Church has no word which could say that this couple should *not* be married, no principle which could possibly be justified under any theory of Christian ethics, that would make their marriage a wrong one. I don't know if you're thinking this, but I imagine you are: Would you want your daughter—? The usual question. I think there's a pretty good answer for that. There are a lot of people I wouldn't want my daughter to marry, including many white people I could think of.

Critic: You'll probably have very little to do with whom she does marry, anyway.

Exponent: Granted. And I imagine the law of averages would be such that the chances are that she would probably meet and marry a white person. On the other hand, we are talking here about free choice in any case, and I don't think that we can wall off the area of choice by imposing limitations on our common community life and on our Church life; this would have the result of

putting whole groups of our fellow Christians in sociological ghettos.

Critic: Now when you advise this couple to be
cautious about inter-racial marriage because of the realities of the situation, weren't you recognizing that there
are certain local facts? I don't think one has to be
prejudiced in order to take this into account. This is
just common sense. And furthermore, isn't it true that
people are more comfortable when they are with their
own group? Isn't this the natural preference?

Exponent: People do prefer to be with the people
they like, but when it comes to artificial barriers that
don't have to do with a particular personality but with
factors such as race, often this preference to be with
one's own—this apparent preference—is a defense
mechanism. Having been forced for so long to have fellowship only with people of one's own color, a de-
fensive reaction has been set up which is not the healthi-
est basis of fellowship even within their own group. So
that even if there is a preference in this direction, Christianity has something to say to that preference—to that
sort of negativism—you might say "inverted" prejudice
—which always develops in an oppressed group.

Critic: This may very well be true, but situations
aren't changed overnight. One of the facts we have to
face is that there *is* such a thing as segregation and a
whole history of segregation, connected with the Negro
people in this country. Now I'd like to raise the question

as to whether or not it isn't better for the Negro people themselves to be given a chance to develop leadership in their own group, without having to be merged into the tough, competitive situation of a mixed racial situation.

Exponent: What you're saying, in other words, is that you think it's better to be a big frog in a little puddle than a little frog in a big puddle.

Critic: That's the general idea.

Exponent: The trouble with this is that such an approach has a permanently retarding effect. The position of the Church that all men are equal under God, works both ways. It means that they not only should have equal benefits, but should be subjected to equal challenges. And if that means during a transitional period that people of the Negro race are not as adequately prepared to respond to these challenges as people of the white race, that in itself will have a stimulating effect for all of us to provide a better groundwork of opportunity —educationally and in terms of love and fellowship— for increasing their native ability. The ability is obviously there: skill is not parcelled out by God only to people of one race. And it will receive its best fulfillment in this very competition you mention. Naturally, equality of opportunity, and opportunity of competitive relationships in fellowship, should begin at the lower grades of education.

Critic: Yes, but in fact it has worked just the other

way around, hasn't it? Non-segregation seems to have started in the graduate schools, and then moved into the colleges; but it hasn't been suggested in the grade schools until very lately.

Exponent: That's true. And that's bad. And unfortunately, the same has been true of the Church. There has long been Negro leadership in the higher councils of our denominational bodies, but we're just beginning to see it here and there on a local parish level.

Critic: But people on the national level of Church organization don't have to live together in a close, day-to-day social situation the way the people in the local churches do. Also, the local church lives in the context of a community situation which has laws that apply to these matters. Even though it might want to rearrange its own life within its church, the Church is still not in a position to change the laws that surround it.

Exponent: You're touching quite a profound point here. But first let me pause to say something about this matter of the local law. First of all, the Church people in a community presumably will have some influence on the actual statutory situation, if they are doing their duty about working to change the law to be more in accord with the will of God.

Critic: What if they can't change it?

Exponent: Then the Church should be in the forefront of those who arrange for challenges of such laws to go up to the Supreme Court. And behind all that is the fact that the Church has never rightfully been in a position to obey the civil law when the civil law violates a profound matter of conscience.

Critic: I suppose it's not really so much the law that's the problem as the power of local customs and popular attitudes. Isn't the solution really to be found on the local level? How can a national Church ever deal with the hard facts of these local attitudes?

Exponent: The very freedom from local problems and local pressures which a national Church body has, or an inter-Church body has, imposes a special responsibility on them to hold the absolute norm before the Church—with charity, to be sure—I mean, recognizing that the local scene differs everywhere, and that these matters do, of course, take time and call for a good deal of internal conversion as well as external arrangement. But the Church in its national public character, or Churches acting together, certainly can represent no compromise in their assertion of principle and in their protest against the evil of segregation, wherever it is found.

Critic: Doesn't that put the Church outside the scope of the realities of existence in this world, then?

Exponent: Precisely. And that is one of the Church's functions. Our Lord bid us be in the world, but not of it. While we must face the realities on the local scene "with the innocence of doves and the wisdom of serpents," we cannot *as the Church* conform to the world or be comfortable in its ways. In a sense, the Church always has to be like the rock in the shoe—or, in more dignified terms, maintain a kind of vertical relationship to the horizontal scene.

Critic: Now, I'm not an officer in the national Church. I operate simply on a local level. At the same time, I have a feeling of responsibility for this question. You've convinced me that this is a real problem and we can't just dismiss it lightly. Now, what can I do—what is my place—in the solution of this problem, in the local situation?

Exponent: Two things: One is to keep constantly open to the vision of brotherhood and fellowship, which is the message of the Church, and seek to apply that locally. The other is to keep those responsible for national leadership alerted as to the actual state of the problem where you are. And together, we may more and more see the day when not only in the Church but in society which is part of what we call a Christian culture, "there is neither Jew nor Greek, there is neither bond nor free, there is neither male nor female: for ye are all one in Christ Jesus."

CHAPTER SIX

"Isn't the Church lagging behind in the elimination of segregation?"

CRITIC: I've been doing a good bit of thinking about the problem of segregation and I've come to the conclusion that this is a real problem and the Church really has a responsibility to do something about it. And this leads me to believe that perhaps there's something in the charges that my more liberal friends have made from time to time, that the Church is much too slow about attacking this problem—that far from being a force in the solution of the problem, the Church is a dead weight holding back progress in the problem of segregation. For example, a friend of mine said to me just the other day that the Church was *the* most segregated institution in our society.

Exponent: Now, wait a minute—there are a lot of other institutions that certainly represent a segregated pattern.

Critic: Let's just look at the situation. In many areas there isn't a college or a university that's segregated, but I know that most parish churches are—in practice.

Exponent: Well, as you know, I'm no defender of segregation; but I think it's only fair to recognize the reason why on the local parish level this matter is more difficult than it is in national church groups or associations, professional associations, colleges or universities. It says a good thing for the Church, actually: the more that a local parish is what it should be—the center of the most intimate fellowship and inter-relationship between people—then the more in fact will be the difficulty of solving the problem of segregation. In other words, people's whole emotional life—I'm including, I'm afraid, their prejudices—can be so tied up with this central experience of the local parish that while such is by no means a good result, it often means that admitting the outsider (or one who through prejudice has long been viewed as the outsider) is more difficult there than simply having someone sit alongside one in a classroom or a professional meeting.

Critic: I can see how this might have a part in the slow progress the Church makes in these matters, but at the same time, doesn't the Church have a responsibility to achieve a higher level of justice than a secular institution such as a college or a social club? You've said before that the Church has a prophetic role to play in society.

Exponent: Yes, it's true that while there is this close and intimate fellowship in a really good parish—which in a sense stands in the way of progress along these lines, a parish church is supposed to have resources of ethical insight and converting power that secular institutions lack—and of course we stand judged on this. But I think it's only fair to point out the tremendous progress that has been made, and made clear that in many areas the Church has been out way ahead of secular society. For example, in the communities where there is complete segregation in education, there is usually not segregation in the synods, presbyteries, diocesan conventions and similar church groups. Also, the Church's seminaries (and sometimes colleges)—even in completely segregated regions, present a non-segregated pattern.

Critic: This is all very encouraging, but I don't see why the authorities of the Church don't just say, "The Church stands against segregation, and this is the way it's going to be," without dilly-dallying around.

Exponent: That's entirely too simple. If the Church were only interested in external conformity, only interested in seeing that those sitting in the pews were sitting in a non-segregated manner, that could be done. And if that was all that the Church was called upon to accomplish, then I would agree with you that it ought to go right ahead and accomplish it and let the chips fall where they may—even with reduced congregations. But the Church's main job is to inspire in individuals a genuine response and willing exercise of redemptive love in a community. And to do this sometimes takes longer. A Church service is not like attendance at a motion picture, where each individual is pretty much on his own and it's only a question of the seating. The achievement of the internal side of this reform is as important as the achievement of the external side.

Critic: Well, doesn't this mean that the total effect of Church life, then, is determined by the average—and a rather mediocre average it is—moral achievement of the people that are involved in it? Shouldn't the Church stand out in society as an institution which is clear-cut in its witness? If people are not ready to make that witness, they shouldn't be in the Church!

Exponent: I'm afraid you're overlooking something that would be embarrassing, perhaps in other realms of activity, to both you and me. The Church is not for the righteous, the Church is for sinners. In one sense, the Church is a hospital. If the Church were to be confined to people who have the right attitudes on everything and behave the right way all the time, it would have an extraordinarily exclusive membership—if indeed it would have any members at all, except the Lord Himself.

Critic: This may be very well in a situation in which the whole culture is informed by Christian principles; in this question of segregation and society, however, the Church finds itself in a culture which can only be described in definitely non-Christian terms. In this kind of a situation, is it ever enough for the Church to say it is just a "hospital for sinners"? Perhaps its role in this case is that of a tightly-knit, well-disciplined protesting minority.

Exponent: In principle this would certainly seem

right. But the trouble is that in terms of practical influence on the community, as the Church becomes smaller and more exclusive it actually has less chance of changing the life of the community than if it can bring along with it and speak for a good many of the half-convinced —*provided* the principles are consistently witnessed to and preached about, and provided that paralleling the efforts to redeem the society around, there is a continuing effort to reach its own members so that their internal responses will match the external changes. I think it's only fair to say that virtually all the progress that has been made toward a better social order in our handling of this problem has stemmed directly or indirectly from the witness and work of the Church. I refer to the work of those ministers who consistently preached against slavery and the constant effort in community after community on the part of the local Council of Churches and of particular ministers to improve the present situation.

Critic: Hasn't a lot of help in this come from people who are outright secularists?

Exponent: It certainly has, and I think that has to be recognized. And yet in a sense, whether they know it or not, they are sort of "fellow-travelers" of the Church's mission in this regard. They are actually informed by principles and ideals which were the Church's in the first place, and which have become the heritage of our secular society as well. Operating on those basic principles, they are making their witness also.

Critic: Yes, but I can't help but feel that if the Church really gave its first attention to this problem, it could move along much faster than it has, both in its own life and in its impact on the community.

Exponent: The Church could give its first attention to the matter, perhaps, but I think we've got to keep the question in perspective. This problem, important as it is, is not the only thing the Church is concerned about. For example, it is very much concerned about maintaining in its own life, and witnessing in the community, to the principles of democracy. In the life of the Church, an authoritarian ukase from on high on such a question may gain ground one way, but there's a loss of ground in another. Furthermore, the Church does hope to keep as many people together in the life of the Church as it can, so that it can nourish the inner life of the individual Christian. This may ultimately give him the strength and courage to do what is right. In any case the Church seeks to hold before him a vision of the Kingdom of God, both as it operates in this world and in the life to come.

Critic: Yes, I can see your point there. But it has distressed me to observe so often that the Church has frequently excused its lack of progress in these matters, and its slowness of action, in its own institutions, by pleading adherence to the civil law.

Exponent: This has distressed me too and yet I think I should say at the outset there is a half-truth in this plea. When I say the Church has a number of things it is supposed to be doing, one of its tasks is to engender respect for the civil law, which is an instrument of God's will on earth, as is the Church's own activity. I would say that the Church does generally say to its members, "Obey the law of the land."

Critic: You mean just any law?

Exponent: No, I said in general. I get the impact of your question, and yet I think at the same time as we assert the patriotic duty to obey the law and thus maintain the structure of the society within which it's possible for the Church to operate, we must also assert that the Church always stands in judgment on any given civil law, especially as it touches deep moral issues. So the Church should continue to work for amendment of legislation which is apparently against the will of God. It has to keep in balance two factors—one which I've already mentioned, the importance of supporting the ordered structure of society, which means that it often has to be patient with situations in society it does not like. On the other hand, if the moral issue is sufficiently important and the Church cannot effect a change in the civil law, then it should disobey it, and encourage its members to do so.

Critic: Mightn't this involve a test in the constitutionality of the law?

Exponent: Yes. And under our system, that really represents the next step.

Critic: What if the Church fails on that?

Exponent: Then the Church still must advise the following of conscience, which may mean disobeying the law even to the point of martyrdom. The Church has a long history on this, you know. We began as a subversive movement in the Roman Empire; the Un-Roman Activities Committee was not at all pleased with our forebears in the faith. The Bible tells us, "It is better to obey God than men." In fact, it's right here that the Church has its most dramatic opportunity to witness to how different the Kingdom of God is—and how different should be those people who are pledged to it—from the secular world in which the Church is set. But I do want to point out one important difference: When a person breaks the law because of some lower claim upon his nature, that's bad and there's no room for that. But when one disobeys the law because of a higher claim upon him, that's obviously a witness to the highest law there is; and in the long run, it forms the basis for the respect for any law.

Critic: Why isn't this point more generally appreciated? Most people in the Church seem to assume that their moral obligation only extends to obeying the law as it is.

Exponent: Well, I think that says a good thing for our society, and the Church, too. Actually, we have had for a long time a Christian society—at least in terms of the structure of ideas which underlay the society, and things had been going along almost too well in regard to the responsiveness of the law to what the Christian ethic seemed to call for. In a way the early Christians were in a much safer situation in this regard, because they knew that the civil law did not necessarily represent *their* best ethical ideals. But the complacency that has been induced in us often blinds us to the fact that the Church goes on and on as cultures rise and fall, and thus its standards can never conform to even a relatively good society any more than it can conform to one that is completely adverse to what the Church stands for in the world.

Critic: I can see that that's part of it. But don't you think that a great many of these "everyday Christians" don't really want the civil law changed, on these matters of segregation?

Exponent: Right you are. And that underlines the importance of emphasizing the Church's dual task. It not only has the task of protest against the wrong kind of social patterns; it has the task of working on the souls of men, to change their motives, and change the directions of their influence. And while this latter approach takes longer, in the long run it's the only way we will achieve that which lies behind our eagerness for a non-segregated society; real fellowship and love and concern rising from the hearts of people toward their fellow men, whatever their race or background.

CHAPTER SEVEN

"Doesn't the Church talk out of both sides of its mouth on the matter of war: pacifistic when we should be preparing and jingoistic when we're actually in a war?"

CRITIC: There's a problem that has been bothering me and bothers a lot of people these days, and that is the problem of war and peace and the place of my conscience in connection with these matters. I don't suppose there has ever been a time in history when the question of what war is going to mean for the world has ever come home to individuals as strongly as it has today. No one can escape facing this question, and a Christian has to face it more acutely than other people. I have been talking to my friends a great deal about this question, and we find ourselves very much confused about the guidance that the Church gives us in this question.

Exponent: Just what do you mean?

Critic: When we come to the Church for an answer we find that it is just as confused as we are. Sometimes the Church talks as if it is strongly pacifistic in its approach to the question of war and peace, and then we find that at other times, when a country becomes involved in the war, the Church comes out very strongly in support of the war and energetic military measures. Flags are carried around, prayers for victory become part of religious services, and preachers plead for support of war as a religious duty.

Exponent: Actually the behavior of the Church on this matter is not as inconsistent as it appears. It is one of the most difficult in the field of Christian ethics and there are no easy answers. In fact, to help focus the problem, let's start with you. If you feel that the Church is about as confused as you are, let's expose your confusion a little bit. What do you really think about the ethics of war?

Critic: Well, obviously, peace is the great ideal. Peace is the thing that we all know is right. On the other hand, there seems to be something in human nature which makes war inevitable. But when I look to the Church for some light on the subject, I seem to hear the Church talking out of both sides of its mouth. On the one hand I hear the Old Testament tell me never to kill, and the New Testament tell me to love my enemies and turn the other cheek, and that if someone takes away my coat I'm supposed to give him my cloak also. I hear quite a different voice coming from the Church at times. I hear, as I said a minute ago, these jingoistic phrases, these impassioned pleas to support the patriotic war. You remember, I'm sure, the phrases that came out of this past war from religious sources, such as "Praise the Lord and pass the ammunition."

Exponent: As a matter of fact, innocently or otherwise you have stated pretty well both sides of the paradox which the Church itself recognizes.

Critic: Is "paradox" just a fancy name for inconsistency?

Exponent: No, a paradox is something that looks inconsistent on the surface but actually isn't, and this very situation is an illustration of it. There can be no question as to what the will of God is for men living in the world together: *Peace* is the will of God and anything other than that involves sin. In the Sermon on the Mount, for example, we have a portrayal of what ideal human life should be, and it is the Church's job always to hold this ideal before men regardless of the actual, practical realities of any given situation. On the other hand, the Church is in the world and is meant to give men real guidance where they are. I am reminded here of the comment that a barking dog never bites but perhaps the dog doesn't know that. The fact is that there are a lot of people in the world who have not so much as heard of the Sermon on the Mount—or, if they have, are not particularly intent on applying it. How we deal with the threat of damage from inimical people is a complicated question.

Critic: Well, you say this is complicated, but I think you make it complicated. Jesus told us very clearly in the New Testament what to do. He said, "Love your enemies and turn the other cheek."

Exponent: That is the ideal thing to do if you are dealing with one-to-one relationships as Jesus was in that discussion. I can turn the other cheek when someone insults me, but in many human situations—and certainly in all the situations which involve the possibility of war —more than two people are involved. If a man insults me I can take the hurt and not hit him back. But suppose he is assaulting a helpless woman when I am standing nearby. Now I have a decision to make between the lesser of two evils. The ideal situation would be that he was not assaulting her; but he *is*. Now if I stand by because of my desire not to hurt him, as enjoined by the Gospel, then I am failing to fulfill my duty to her; and in actual result I am on his side in the harm that is done to her. I have to decide between hurting him—which, as such, is undesirable—and letting a helpless person be hurt because of his ill will.

Critic: Why not call a policeman?

Exponent: Suppose he comes. You have the same problem all over again. His very existence indicates a decision that there are circumstances in which, in a less than ideal world, we choose to hurt people as the lesser of two evils. Now this same thing applies in the question of even a world war. Let's take the last one, and the position the United States was put in. If at the time of Pearl Harbor the choice was war or peace, then obviously peace is the answer. That wasn't the choice we had. The choice we had was war with one kind of outcome or war with another kind of outcome.

Critic: In other words, you are saying that the choice was between a war in which we would be victorious or a war in which we would be subjugated. Now, doesn't this put it on a purely selfish basis?

Exponent: No, there is much more involved than that. If there was a choice between a war in which, with the victory of the authoritarian forces the possibility of a free society would have been over in the world, and a war in which the outcome would leave the possibility of human freedom—now this is saying more than that our nation is a good nation and the Germans under Hitler or the Japanese under Tojo were bad nations.

Critic: Yes, there certainly is plenty wrong with us, too.

Exponent: That's right. But our heritage and constitutional set-up is such that there is at least a chance of doing something about it, of remedying by free processes those evil aspects of our own society which disturb the Christian conscience, whereas under authoritarianism such opportunities are over. But my point is this: *that* was the choice before us. The third possibility, that is, of peace, was not one of the possible choices. Here the Christian conscience, confronted with only two choices, must be realistic about the choices—in fact, open—and must not behave as though this third choice, namely, of peace, is really open. Naturally, then, the Church got behind the war effort, choosing what was actually the lesser of two evils.

Critic: Well, I'm still not clear just what this has to do with *Christian* ethics. It seems to me that what you're saying is that when such choices are forced upon us we are simply to make them on the grounds of expediency. What does the Christian point of view or the Christian message have to say about this at all? Certainly a lot of people who aren't Christians could have made the same choice with the same sense of expediency.

Exponent: Indeed they might have, and in fact did. But remember the Christian Church is very much interested in our motivations for choice and what we're like after having made the choice. If we simply decide to go to war against the enemy because we want our side to win, that does one thing to us. If, on the other hand, we go to war against the enemy knowing that we're *all* partly in the wrong, but that greater harm to the world will come from their victory than from ours, we have a proper humility under God. In a sense we go to war beating our breast and saying, "Lord, have mercy upon us."

Critic: Isn't the only result of this breast-beating that you talk about to weaken the moral fibre and the determination of the soldier? Wouldn't he be a better soldier if he just threw himself into the business of war without such qualms of conscience?

Exponent: Not necessarily. We aren't saying that he should fight less vigorously. Once we have determined that a particular outcome is nearer to the will of God, or at least less far from the will of God than another outcome, then, as Christians, we are called to throw our entire weight behind the effort.

Critic: All right, then. Suppose the Christian soldier does this, goes into war this way. Isn't the enemy soldier he shoots just as dead as if he'd been shot by a soldier of unqualified super-patriotism?

Exponent: Certainly. But there are two differences. Remember, we're concerned always with the individual. There is a difference in the kind of spiritual life and relationship to God of the soldier who perceives that he's caught in a guilty situation as he acts, and one who is blind to this point. And in terms of the outcome, the kind of peace that's apt to be made will be a sounder one if the victorious nation has all along recognized its involvement in the guilt of war rather than if it has had an unqualified sense of self-righteousness throughout.

Critic: Well, I think I see your point. But there's something you said a while back that I'd like to talk about some more. You said that in the actual situation the individual person was not given the opportunity to choose absolute peace. He can only choose between two evils. But doesn't the pacifist actually make this his choice? He chooses the way of peace by simply refraining from taking any part in the war.

Exponent: It appears so. But no man is an island to himself. His nation in fact is in a war and his situation is affected by it. In the illustration I used earlier, of where the man stood by and watched a tough fellow beat up a helpless woman, his very inaction was a decision. Likewise, in wartime, when a man stands by and is not counted in the effort against great evil in the world, in a sense that's just that much for the other side. In any case, he profits from the victory of his nation that he has not participated in. Suppose he has some investments; the value that accrues to him from earnings on stock in, say, a steel company will doubtless be greater. He cannot really divorce himself from the whole scene around him.

Critic: Then do you think that the pacifist position is never justifiable?

Exponent: No, I don't think that. Some people are called to make a witness to the absolute demands of the Kingdom of God, to make a witness to the image of peace that always should be kept before the world even in the midst of the bloodiest war. But my concern is that such a man does not do so in a self-righteous way, feeling that he has chosen the higher life as it were. In making his special witness he should realize that he, too, is involved in the world in which he lives and is not in a perfectly unstained situation in regard to the ebb and flow of the war picture.

Critic: What you mean is that pacifism is all right as long as there aren't too many pacifists. If too many people have this idea of a kind of lofty witness to the peace ideal it would soon weaken our manpower for the prosecution of a war.

Exponent: Well, I'm afraid you've stated it about right. It's good to have some people making this witness, but we can't afford to have too many. And in fact there's never been a war in which we have had.

Critic: I take it that you do mean then that in general people ought just to fall in line behind whatever decision their country has made in regard to going to war.

Exponent: No, it's not that simple. When I talk about the lesser of two evils I am not merely talking in terms of what the nation should decide, I am thinking of the individual's responsibility as well. I think every individual has the responsibility when war is threatened to decide as best he can whether going to war or not is the lesser of the two evils. In other words, it's possible that his nation might declare war in a situation in which he conscientiously feels that his nation is wrong. Now this same man may not be a pacifist in an abstract or general sense, but he would for this particular war be a pacifist.

Critic: What kind of a situation do you have in mind?

Exponent: Take this example—which is partially hypothetical but not entirely so. Let's assume that we were living at the time of the Mexican War and that a draft was imposed. Let's assume further that we then knew as much as we now know about the Mexican War.

Critic: Well, I see the point of that qualification because in the heat of the moment it's very hard to get at such facts.

Exponent: Yes. Now it would seem that this was a fairly unjustified war of aggression, simply to appropriate additional lands, and where our national security was not threatened in any way. In such a case I think it would be the duty of the Christian to refuse to participate in such a war.

Critic: The only difficulty with this position is that a general, abstract, doctrinaire pacifism gives you a draft exemption from military duty, while this selective pacifism which you describe would be called treason.

Exponent: Right you are. But we're talking about the Christian conscience, and often through the history of the Church the Christian conscience has been compelled to take positions which a government has regarded as traitorous. Treason or no, under the facts the Christian would have to stand aside.

Critic: On your theory is it enough for him just to stand aside? Shouldn't he be taking some active steps?

Exponent: You're right. And this is true of all pacifist attitudes whether they are simply applied to a particular war situation or whether they represent a general position. And in fairness to those who do take a general pacifist position, they do feel that their duty is more than just standing aside. They feel called upon to take an active part in the whole matter, principally in terms of seeking to persuade our fellow citizens, and through all of us the Government, not to engage in the war at all.

Critic: I take it by your reference to such an obscure example as the Mexican War that you think that in general this country has engaged in just wars.

Exponent: No, I'd hesitate to use the word "just" war. There is a tradition in Christian theology that uses this phrase. But I think it would be more correct to say that no war is really a just war. The best we can say about a war—and I feel in conscience we can say this about, for example, the last world war—is that getting into the war seems to offer the likelihood of an outcome in which there will be more justice and grace to operate in the world than if we don't get into the war. That seems the most that we can say. But in terms of a realistic Christian ethic I think if we can say that, then we can say that the decision we make is to get into the war.

Critic: I'm beginning to see that the question is resolved in terms of paradox rather than mere inconsistency. However, there is one thing that occurs to me. All of your examples and your statements on these questions we've been discussing have come from past history—from wars in the past. Now, don't we find ourselves today in a very different situation in the light of the development of new and much more comprehensive, horrible weapons of war than were ever available to man in the past? I'm referring to the H-bomb and the cobalt bomb—and worse to come.

Exponent: I don't think that this presents a new ethical situation; it simply changes the factual situation that has to be taken into account if any balance of factors is made. It is true that if, to right some wrong in the world, we get into a war which would seem inevitably to involve us in the use of atomic weapons, it would be much harder than in the past to come to the conclusion that we have chosen the lesser of two evils. We might feel that letting certain unjust and even intolerable situations continue is a lesser evil than destroying half of the face of the earth or, for all we know, destroying all human life on the earth. In other words, the principle doesn't change; the facts have changed.

Critic: Do you mean to say that in Christian ethics you see no absolute bar to the use of nuclear weapons?

Exponent: I'm afraid I can't, as an absolute bar. Let's trace the thing back to primitive times. If it's wrong to kill a man by throwing a rock at him, and yet, in self-defense or defense of helpless people, doing so would be regarded as the lesser of two evils, the *principle* doesn't change when we move up through pistols and cannons and block-busters which can destroy thousands of people at a time. But our horror—a very proper horror in a Christian civilization at such mass destruction

—should remind us that the factors on the other side have to be enormous before we dare even presume to think that a lesser of two evils would be involved in the use of such weapons. In fact, it almost comes down to necessity because we have been attacked first or are in imminent danger of attack by atomic weapons. It would be a very terrible decision to have to make. That is why all the more the Christian conscience in this field should alert us to the most constant and active efforts to establish peace in the world.

Critic: One thing that gives me some uneasiness in the position you've stated is that you don't seem to be trusting God to make things right in the long run. You seem to be implying that national existence here and now, or personal survival on the part of individuals here and now, is the crucial thing. Doesn't the Christian teaching in the end say that we can and must make a choice of an absolute white rather than an expedient choice between two shades of grey, since, after all, there is eternal life, even though all might be lost here and that God would make things right in eternity.

Exponent: God does make things right in eternity; but here and now is part of eternity, and God cares what happens here and now. God does care for the preservation of the best possibilities in this world, even if they are not complete possibilities for justice and grace. God does care what happens to the best values of our civilization. He does *not* depend upon them, nor does our fulfillment finally depend upon the structures of our common life here and now, but these structures, in so far as they are good and a partial reflection of the eternal Kingdom of God, are things that we are called upon as Christians to seek earnestly to preserve. Oddly enough, this paradox between eternity and life here and now is rather pointed up by the presence of clergy serving as chaplains in the armed forces.

Critic: Well, that's true. Men did go into the chaplaincy during the last war because they felt there were greater possibilities for good in our victory than there would be in our defeat. But what about chaplaincies in military establishments in peacetime? How can the Church justify that?

Exponent: On quite simple grounds. As a matter of fact, the matter of chaplaincies in war or peace is much simpler than the problem facing a Christian in deciding whether he should serve as an armed member of the military personnel. The Church is called upon to minister to people wherever they are, whether they ought to be in the situation or not. After all, we have chaplaincies in penitentiaries, whose inmates presumably shouldn't have gotten themselves there. That doesn't mean we are justifying crime. In other words, even in this Mexican War illustration we used, it would have been quite suitable for a chaplain to go along to minister to the spiritual needs of the men. Certainly with the tremendous dislocation of large elements of our society due to large-scale draft, the Church has to rearrange its personnel to minister to these large numbers of people who rather especially need ministry in a transition stage of their lives.

CHAPTER EIGHT

"What business have our Churches imposing their religion on people in countries with other faiths?"

CRITIC: Since our discussion of the problem of war and peace, I've been wondering if the missionary program of the Churches, in attempting to impose our particular religious outlook on other cultures, doesn't contribute to world tension.

Exponent: This is a large subject, but right away I must object to the use of your word "impose" in connection with the missionary effort, at least in modern circumstances.

Critic: What are you hiding in that last phrase?

Exponent: Well, I will grant that at times in the past when a Church combined its missionary effort with imperial ambitions of a nation, the religion was in effect imposed upon the people, particularly if they became a subject people. But this is past history. There is no place in the world where the missionary program in any way could or does seek to impose the Christian faith upon the people to whom it is preached.

Critic: What is the aim then?

Exponent: The aim is to present Christianity attractively in a variety of ways; through social service, education, and the direct teaching of Christianity, in the hope that people in these various countries may be persuaded to accept its truths.

Critic: I am glad to see that you admit that in times past, at any rate, the Church has been guilty of identifying its missionary program with the political and economic imperialism of a nation. But I wonder if the Churches are as free from this accusation now as they think they are. The Churches sometimes engage in what might be called a cultural imperialism, which can be just as imperious as any other kind of imperialism.

Exponent: Certainly there is nothing more insidious about it than there is about the attempt of Americans to acquaint these people with the results of modern science, modern machinery, modern journalism, modern entertainment—all of which have come from our part of the world.

Critic: But I am not at all sure that there is too much in our modern machinery and modern entertainment that is desirable for a people of another culture.

Exponent: I will agree with you there, especially if in exporting these other things we don't export along with them the religious and ethical attitudes which have enabled us, in a measure at least, to live with them. It seems to me that we should be more eager to export good ideas, particularly as touching the spirit and ethical insights of man, than to export things.

Critic: Why should insights and ideas which are good in our culture necessarily be good for people in another culture? After all, religious beliefs consistent with their whole cultural situation have been serving these people for generations.

Exponent: There is much in what you say. In any case, the task of the missionary is not to destroy the religious insights or even the religious customs of any people. Any truth in Buddhism, for example, is of God because all truth is God's truth. There are insights as to mysticism and a quality of spirituality in many people raised with Oriental religions which certainly must be treasured. More than that, the words and ideas that are appropriate in expressing religion in the West may not be at all appropriate in expressing the Christian faith in the East.

Critic: Can you give me an example?

Exponent: Well, for example: in our Apostles' Creed, we say that Jesus "sitteth on the right hand of God." Obviously this won't go at all in a country where the place of honor is the left hand of the host; thus the Creed is modified in bringing it to such people. This is a very trivial example of a more profound rethinking of all the words and ideas that goes on in the attempt to transplant Christianity elsewhere.

Critic: You mentioned that religious *practices* can even be preserved.

Exponent: Yes. In a Christian church in India, for example, people don't kneel for prayer; they sit cross-legged; and they take off their shoes at the door. It is no longer in fashion for missionaries nostalgically to build a "carpenter's gothic" church in the shadow of the Himalayas. Bishops in the Church of South India don't wear black, which the Hindus associate with evil—but saffron, which they associate with holiness. And even as to matters of belief, we really want to *add* the insights of Christianity to what they already have rather than to take something away.

Critic: Do you mean to say that there is no conflict between Christianity and these other faiths at any point —that Christianity is just added on top?

Exponent: No, I don't mean to say that where there *are* conflicts. For example, the Oriental religions generally think of an unconscious after-life, while Christianity believes in a personal conscious life beyond the grave.

Critic: What happens when there is such a conflict?

Exponent: Then the two ideas simply have to compete in the market-place of thought and the people decide for themselves.

Critic: But what right have we to say that in such cases of conflict the faith that we have is superior for these people to that which has come out of their own history and their own culture?

Exponent: The same way that our country through various official and unofficial means has tried to tell the world beyond the Iron Curtain that our way of government is the right way and that theirs is slavery. What we believe we proclaim to the world.

Critic: Because we have experienced democracy we know that it's better than forms of government that deprive us of freedom. But when it comes to religion, we haven't had quite the same kind of experience. Religion is something that's more spiritual. Religion has to do with things that are supernatural—about which we can't prove anything anyway.

Exponent: Oh, I object there. I think the right kind of religion affords the same basis of experience as does our experience with the freedom in democracy. Where men have known a new spiritual freedom, a new confidence, healing and release through the Christian faith, they know its truth just the same way that a person can know the merits of a free society. The trouble with some of the people who object to Missions is that the Christian faith has not been really experienced personally by them in their lives; they haven't relied upon it for their strength, and do not know its power, and hence they can see no particular reason why, as a body of ideas, it is a better set of truths than what the non-Christians hold.

Critic: But what right have I to think, and what right have our Churches to think, that our experience of religion in our culture is any more convincing to us than their experience of religion is to them?

Exponent: The point might be very well taken were it not for the fact that we can, looking at the course of the world's history, see objectively some of the differences in the effect of Christianity and the other religions upon men's lives and in their possession of the worth-while things of life. For example, it has been only out of the Judaeo-Christian heritage that there has been any concept of progress at all, and there is now a concern for continued progress in bettering men's conditions in other non-Christian lands only through the influence of Christianity directly or of the way of life which has sprung from the Judaeo-Christian roots.

Critic: It sounds very materialistic when our chief claim for religion is based on the number of *things* people have.

Exponent: Well, I do profess a materialistic religion. I think it was William Temple who pointed out that Christianity is the most materialistic of religions. We do believe it is the will of God that people, through their ingenuity and cooperativeness and progress, have things which make life happier for them. But I wouldn't stop there. Let's consider the place of women in the world. Their equality and dignity is due to the Christian influence in the world. The concept of marriage and the home and the relation of children and their parents is another example.

Critic: But isn't this just what Christian missionaries always do: they go into a country where it has been the custom from time immemorial for people who are good citizens to have families based on three, four, five or any number of wives and impose the Christian idea of one wife. Doesn't this create tensions?

Exponent: Certainly, during the transition period; but I think you would concede that the fullest development of personal relationships depends upon monogamy. Monogamy isn't just a question of one custom versus another. For two persons to be related in a mutual way with the fullest involvement of personalities, monogamy has a place that I think anyone can see represents a higher level of human relationships.

But let's take the whole matter of altruism, the notion that people ought to be concerned for the unfortunate, the spread of hospitals and orphanages and the like.

Critic: Don't missionaries really use these activities as bait in order to get their other teachings across?

Exponent: As a matter of fact, I don't think that's altogether what it is. The eagerness of our missionaries to establish hospitals and homes for the homeless and so forth is simply the natural reaction of Christians to a situation in which there's widespread misfortune. It goes back to my previous point that without the centuries of a Christian outlook on things, the sick have been untended for generations and the unfortunate have been given very little care. Hence the Church tends to make almost its first job to meet the need of the neighbor. The Good Samaritan is not pictured as giving a lecture on Samaritan theology—as contrasted to Jewish theology—to the man who had fallen among thieves; rather he rushed him to an inn. I think Christianity is displayed in its most characteristic attitude in the way that modern missionary methods put such emphasis on the meeting of the needs of the people.

Critic: What happens then when these peoples develop educationally to such an extent that they have their own hospitals, their own doctors and nurses? What need for Christianity is there then?

Exponent: The hope always, not only in mission lands but in our own land, is that the Church can, as it were, prime the pump for these activities and that gradually they will become the characteristic activities of the society itself. But meanwhile, it is hoped that Christianity has made an impression on the inner life of those whom it is serving. Anyway a Christian hospital is not something separate from the church: in fact, the first hospitals in the Christian era were simply churches with beds surrounding the center of worship. But in any case, Christianity does not think that the full need of man is met when his body has been well tended or his stomach filled.

Critic: From what you have said I can see that practically speaking there may be some point in missionary activity. It *is* a good thing to develop hospitals and build schools and meet the practical needs of people in a spirit of charity; provided our churches don't introduce any dogma into their work!

Exponent: Well, I was about to feel that we had

reached the end of this discussion on a very amicable basis, but that last proviso troubles me. "Dogmatic" in the sense of being intolerant or unwilling to listen or see what good there is in another position—that we don't want on the part of the Church or of anybody else. But in another sense, when we say "dogma," we mean a conviction held about a serious matter, and the Church in that sense must always be dogmatic, because it does have definite convictions about the meaning of life which are not just derived from trial-and-error or experience, important as it is that religion be experienced. But you see, Christianity makes a unique claim. It claims that it is something revealed to men by God acting from outside of history, expressing Himself in history. The real reason why we feel we must bring the Gospel to all parts of the world is that we feel we are under a commission to do so. Our Lord told us to preach the Gospel to every creature.

Critic: But didn't Jesus tell His disciples in another place to go first in their work to the house of Israel, seeming to indicate that He regarded His message as something for a particular culture?

Exponent: He did, of course, in His earthly ministry, as a Jew living among His own people and feeling primarily responsibility for those around Him—which, by the way, must be the primary responsibility for Christians in any given community today. But when the fullness of the revelation came to pass in His Resurrection, then He made very evident the universal claims of Christianity. It is from the period after the Resurrection that comes the word, "Go ye therefore and make disciples of all nations, baptizing them in the name of the Father and of the Son and of the Holy Ghost." Then, further, He intended this mission to go on right through history because the passage is completed with these words: "Lo, I am with you alway, even unto the end of the world."

Critic: Isn't this just to say that Jesus, like any great teacher, wanted His ideas spread?

Exponent: It says a great deal more than that to the Christian. The very heart of our message is that Jesus Christ is more than a great teacher. To us He is God Incarnate, God giving us a final expression *in our terms* of His meaning for us. To surrender this point, which is really the fundamental basis of our missionary effort, is to surrender Christianity itself.

Critic: Isn't Christianity itself a divided message? We present the spectacle of competing Christian groups accusing each other before these people whom we are trying to convert.

Exponent: You are partially right and partially wrong in your assessment of the situation. There is no question but what these divisions are a scandal—in the original meaning of the word, a "stumbling block." It is not a scandal particularly associated with the missionary movement; it is a scandal of a divided Christendom in the world as a whole. One of the reasons why Christians are so earnestly working through the World Council of Churches and the ecumenical movement generally, as well as in conversations between particular denominations, for a greater measure of church unity, is that we are all too aware of the fact that by our divisions we hamper the work of the Holy Spirit in converting men to Christ. The Lord anticipated this very thing in His great high priestly prayer the night He was betrayed. He said that He wasn't praying for His present disciples alone, "but for them also which shall believe through their word, that they all may be one in us: that the world may believe that Thou has sent me. . . ."

Critic: But you said I was partially wrong in my criticism of the competing sects.

Exponent: Yes, I think that there is an important thing you overlook. All through the centuries Christian men have sincerely disagreed about certain emphases and certain interpretations of the Christian Gospel.

Critic: Should that be allowed?

Exponent: You sound like an Inquisitor of a bygone era. There was a time when it wasn't allowed; and those were not better times, at least as to this matter. And there are places today, such as Spain and Colombia, where it isn't allowed; and these are not good places, at least as to this matter. The freedom to espouse one's own version of Christianity is a valuable right; and that very opportunity for divergence among sincere people provides a good lesson for the cultures to which Christianity is being brought.

Critic: Who are we to presume to take Christianity to other countries and other cultures? We are far from being a Christian nation ourselves.

Exponent: A good point, indeed, and I think this gives us a measure of humility about the whole matter which sometimes we lack in referring to ourselves as a "Christian nation." But isn't the answer to that problem *both/and*, not *either/or*? We will not improve our own Christianity if that Christianity is not viewed as missionary. In its very nature, Christianity is something that puts a challenge on people to spread it. We have to regard our own nation as a mission, too. The relation of the two things can be illustrated by the fact that the light which shines farthest is the one that is brightest at the source. There is more to be said: Actually, we may see the time when the newer, younger Churches will be sending missionaries to us to help complete the task. That is, we are not just on the giving side, as anyone knows that has heard the preaching in this country of some of the native Christians in other lands who have assumed leadership in the Church there. Some of the great leaders in the ecumenical movement itself, in the World Council, are those who have come out of what you would call non-Christian cultures, cultures for which you apparently didn't think Chritianity was very suitable.

Critic: But, after all, aren't we all going to the same place eventually? People of these other faiths are simply going by different routes.

Exponent: The only difficulty with that comment is that no Moslem would think so. You are imposing your ideas on people of other religions yourself. For example, as to "going the same place," the Hindu or Buddhist believes that life after death at its best is dissolution of the personality, whereas Christianity teaches that it is fulfillment of the personality in free and intimate fellowship with God and His saints. In fact, not all forms of Christianity teach that all *Christians* are going to the same place. In any case, to speak more seriously, what kinds of persons we'll be when we get to this place has to do with what kind of spiritual life we have known *here* and what guidance and grace we have had.

Critic: Do you mean to say that God isn't providing light and guidance to the people in other religions?

Exponent: I wouldn't say that at all. God's ways are very mysterious and He operates in a much wider way than the particular channels He has revealed to us. But the principal way He does bring light and guidance and grace to them is through those to whom He has revealed Himself in Jesus Christ. We are called to be God's agents or means of grace to these people, which is a great burden and responsibility upon us. Thus our failure to serve Him adequately in this way—and to serve them—is a judgment indeed upon us.

CHAPTER NINE

"Isn't the Church, because of its dogmatism, really an enemy of freedom in the world?"

CRITIC: I've been hearing a good many sermons of late on the subject of freedom and democracy and a great many of these sermons have attributed our freedom to our religion. There's something that troubles me about this, however. It seems to me that religion is based in the long run on dogmas and dogmatism. Now, how can something that is inherently dogmatic, such as religion, really be a source of freedom? In fact, a number of my friends think that because of this very dogmatism, religion is the enemy of freedom.

Exponent: You've opened a big subject. Before we really get into it, I'd just like to make one surface observation. The fact is that the only places in the world where real working democracies, as we know them, have arisen have been in cultures drenched with Christian belief. So, whatever we get into in our discussion about the theory of the thing, that's the fact of it. Apparently Christianity has not in effect been such an enemy of freedom.

Critic: I know this has been true of some countries. But on the other hand, there have been other countries that have been called Christian, which have had very little freedom or democracy at all.

Exponent: Well, as you know, there are different kinds of Christianity. Some encourage freedom more than do others. But I don't want to get into that yet, till we handle some more basic things. First of all, you use this word "dogma" as a kind of a nasty word, and I'll admit that is pretty generally the way it is used in this country these days. But tell me what you really think a dogma is so that we'll know what we're talking about.

Critic: I suppose I've always thought a dogma means accepting something on authority that you can't prove.

Exponent: Strictly speaking, most of our basic working ideas, the value patterns we have, the assumptions we make about the world we're in, are things we can't really *prove*. And as far as authority goes, all of our assumptions and our acceptance of even particular facts rest upon a number of kinds of authority: our own personal experience, the experience of other people whom we trust, a long tradition, or what we may believe is word from on high on a subject. I would define a dogma as being a conviction seriously held on a matter that is ultimately important, and we all have such convictions whether we are humanists or materialists, Marxists, or what not.

Critic: What you would say then is that there are both good and bad dogmas.

Exponent: That's right. And a religion is to be judged by how good its dogmas are, as is any other position that people hold and operate with in their daily lives.

Critic: I still don't care much for this word *dogma*, but I would certainly agree that people must have convictions. There's a difference, however, between convictions that are received from some church and a conviction that has been wrought out through personal experience and the struggle of choice.

Exponent: I agree with you on this. I believe a time should come in the life of every adult, whatever his religious background or lack of the same, when he thinks through the ground of what he really can believe and what seems really meaningful to him, and chooses on this basis his religious allegiance; and ——

Critic: Well, then you have him right back in a strait-jacket again.

Exponent: But you see it's not a strait-jacket under those circumstances. If he just believes what he was taught and he has never thought it through, that's one thing. But if he has thought it through and ends up holding a certain set of convictions, and then gets into an outfit that holds those convictions and, as it were, holds up the banner of this particular tradition because he sincerely believes that those ideas should be furthered in the world, then this has been on a basis of free choice.

Critic: This may be true of certain religious traditions, but what would you say of Roman Catholicism or Fundamentalism?

Exponent: It's true there too. If a person decides to become a Roman Catholic it is because he decides to believe the set of dogmas which make up Roman Catholicism. If a man decides to join one of the fundamentalist sects, it is because he believes that he can sincerely believe everything in the Bible as it is literally written. Now perhaps the point you're getting at is that in other traditions there are not so many dogmas or beliefs that make up the set of basic convictions, and that is certainly true. But in any case, whether the dogmas involved be few or many, a man is making a free choice when he becomes or remains a particular kind of Christian.

Critic: This may be true in theory, but in practice does such a choice actually occur, particularly for people who are born and brought up in a certain dogmatic religious tradition?

Exponent: It may not, and when this period of questioning never occurs in a person's life, it often means that they're not really religiously serious, regardless of what religion they may profess. But with a good many people, either a tragedy in life or an approaching marriage or a maturing of thought in other realms causes a kind of period of doubt and questioning which results in that person's either coming to believe in another tradition or re-accepting his own tradition in a deeper way.

Critic: Well, I think I can go along with you on this

matter of the freedom implied or involved in making the
initial choice between one religious tradition and another. But I wonder if, having made that choice, the
person is left free, in the light of the dogmatic structure
that he has accepted, to engage from time to time in continuing criticism of the belief itself.

Exponent: Of course he should be. In fact, important events in his life, or new information, or conversations with people, or a book that he reads, or new
insights—any one of these things may cause him to stop
and rethink a particular position. If the alteration is sufficient that he can no longer sincerely retain the particular
denominational allegiance, then he ought to make a
change. On the other hand, a number of the Churches
leave room for a great deal of difference of emphasis and
of opinion about a good many things about which one
can ask religious questions, just as did the early Christian
Church. However, it is not very practical for a man constantly to call his basic convictions into criticism. Life
must move on, and a man's faith is the ground under his
feet. For example, a man and a woman may spend some
time deciding whether to get married. But after they are
married, only the rudest jolt to their affections or the
most basic sort of disagreement or infidelity is going
to cause either to raise the basic question, "Do I want
to be married to this person?" One *is* married to the
other. Within that relationship there is room for a certain measure of freedom of opinion or even of estimate

of each other, but the relationship nevertheless is assumed. The point is that if people really take their religion seriously and are thinking about it and applying it to life, they are constantly going to be getting new light and they are going to be discarding inadequate conceptions of God and of the eternal realities. The freedom of man so to do in a basic religious framework is to me a rather important element in the choice of what particular kind of Christian a man wants to be.

Critic: You think it is proper, then, for a Christian to take seriously modern Biblical criticism which in many cases calls into question dates, authorship, and even the content of the various books of the Bible?

Exponent: Certainly he should take all that seriously. All truth is God's truth, and the Christian should hide from nothing that is supported by factual truth. After all, the Christian's basic convictions are not dependent upon any particular matter of Biblical authorship or date, or even upon particular quotations from Scripture.

Critic: Well, there has to be a foundation somewhere. What is the unassailable content of the Christian faith, then?

Exponent: I'm glad you asked that question because I think sometimes Christians themselves have not always carefully distinguished essentials from non-essentials in this regard. Obviously Abraham didn't come into Palestine with a copy of the Pentateuch under his arm, and obviously St. Paul did not go around the Mediterranean distributing pocket Testaments. Yet Abraham had a religion to live by and St. Paul had a message to preach. Behind the words of Scripture is a faith. And the books of Scripture were regarded by the Church—the Old Israel and the New Israel—as the best expression of the faith already held.

Critic: What is this basic faith then?

Exponent: It is the conviction that God is and has acted in history, and it is a recital of the mighty acts of God on behalf of us men and our salvation. Perhaps the most terse way to sum it up is to say it's what any one of the Apostles preached when he got a chance to talk in a synagogue—It was the good news he was announcing.

Critic: What were those early sermons that the Apostles preached?

Exponent: We find scattered through the New Testament sort of "Reader's Digest summaries" of these early sermons, the memory of which the Christians treasured. They all ran something like this: God who had made all things had great expectations of us, and we hadn't lived up to those expectations and were in sin and need. And He came among us, translating Himself into the language of a human life. He taught and healed men, and then took upon Himself the burden of our sins, hurts, and frustrations, even to the death of the cross. But He rose victorious from the grave and reigns on high, thus sanctifying our humanity, and continuing to work in and through us by the Holy Spirit in the life of the Church, bringing the promise of life eternal to all of us who are willing to join ourselves to this movement among men designed to save them.

Critic: That sounds very much like a free paraphrase of the Apostles' Creed.

Exponent: Exactly! I was trying in a way almost to disguise that fact at this point in our conversation. The early creeds of the Church do sum up these great verbs of God's action.

Critic: Well, the creeds get us right back to dogma again, don't they? And if we are committed to a dogmatic message such as you have described, then it's very difficult for me to see how we can say that freedom has been engendered by all of this.

Exponent: To narrow the question down, I must say first that one is still free in even the broad sense, that is, free to accept all this or not. But your feeling is that if you do accept it, then you're no longer free. Do I understand you aright?

Critic: Yes, that's my point.

Exponent: Accepting any such system of thought would be a form of bondage if one's loyalty were to the creeds themselves. But one accepts and recites the creeds because they seem to him to express the affirmations that belong to his loyalty to something that lies beyond the creeds, namely, to Christ Himself.

Critic: But doesn't this subservience to Christ, who,

after all, was a historical figure living in a particular place and time in history, mean that you are thereby robbed of your freedom to be a free person capable of looking at all of life in a free creative way, taking into account the universal insights of mankind?

Exponent: You forget that for the Christian, when we're dealing with Christ, we're dealing with God, who is over and above time and place. What we see in Christ is what are the universal meanings for man and the picture of how God deals with all men who will let Him deal with them. We're here right at the crux of this whole matter. I think it was Søren Kierkegaard who bade us have absolute relationship to what is absolute, and only relative relationships to the things that are relative. In other words, if God alone is our absolute loyalty, then we are freed to sit loose to all else, and thus even free to look critically at the teaching and behavior of the Church itself at any given time in history.

Critic: Well, you say this, but my reading of church history suggests that the Church itself hasn't always encouraged this kind of freedom you mention.

Exponent: I must confess that it hasn't. This is one sign of its human character. The taking of criticism gracefully isn't an easy matter for fallen man, and sometimes the higher one's ecclesiastical dignity the more difficult this seems to be. But at the heart of at least one form of Christianity is the concept that self-criticism and criticism of all human institutions, even ecclesiastical ones, is part of what we mean by God's absolute primacy, and this is the meaning of that peculiar role in the Church known as the reformer.

Critic: You can hardly give the Church credit for the reformers. The Church did everything it could to extinguish them.

Exponent: That is true in one sense but in another sense you *must* give the Church credit for the reformer. We must remember that Martin Luther wasn't a man from Mars or from an oriental culture; he was an Augustinian monk who had learned about the Bible and St. Paul and St. Augustine—on whom he so much relied— right within the life of the Church. He was saying his prayers daily and participating in the Eucharist with his brethren, and out of this experience came the insights which caused him, if I may use the phrase, to make an end-run around the Church and stand on God's side in judgment against the Church.

Critic: But didn't Martin Luther really challenge dogmas? Or anyway, he wanted new and different dogmas.

Exponent: No, as a matter of fact he didn't. I don't want to argue out the Lutheran Reformation, or any other, at this point. But I will say this: every reformer, rightly or wrongly, has thought that he was returning to the fountainhead of Christian belief as against what had been intervening distortions of the Christian faith. And this is at least one of the most important reasons for having a system of belief in the Church which is witnessed-to corporately throughout the centuries. From time to time, when there have been distortions either in the way of stating doctrines or in practice of behavior, the fountainhead can be examined again and those things continuously and universally believed by the Church compared to deviations which have distorted the basic frame.

Critic: Well, I must say, you make the role of the reformer—which, incidentally, reminds me very much of the Old Testament prophet in his work—very attractive indeed. But I wonder if the Church itself is as ready to recognize the value of this kind of person.

Exponent: That depends upon the given tradition within Christianity. Our time here will not permit going into all of that. But important to many Christian groups is the affirmation of the direct relationship of the individual to God and the individual's responsibility for his own life and the integrity of his decisions within the general structure of the basic Christian faith. This encouragement of the freedom of the Christian man to speak his mind honestly not only from the outside looking in, but within the life of the Church, is a characteristic mark of many of our Christian bodies.

Critic: It's good to know that this kind of freedom and this principle exist within many Church traditions. But I still wonder just what this has to do with political freedom, the essentials of a free democracy.

Exponent: Well, here is the connection. When people in the deepest levels of their experience—that is, their religious life—get used to dealing directly with God and feel that He is the one sure thing, then they get accustomed to sitting loose to all else, and aren't ready to take anything else, finally speaking, on authority— much as they may respect authority. This is why people in the religious tradition which has most stressed this individual relationship to God have been able in their cultures to produce democracies. There is a positive side to it too: it is not simply the sitting loose to all forms of authoritarian control; it's also that placing a strong degree of responsibility upon the individual under God gives the inner controls to life that make corporate life possible in some degree of cohesiveness with the interposition of a minimum of external authority.

Critic: I should think that habit of mind would be a very good defense against Communism.

Exponent: Right you are. Not simply the Church's *talking* against Communism; it's the habit of mind, the temper of spirit, the growth in this kind of responsibility under God. That's the best defense against Communism. That is why, though the Churches influenced by this Reformation tradition we've been talking about may not talk against Communism more than other groups, in fact Communism has not gotten a hold or had any substantial following in any of the countries which have been primarily influenced over the years by this single religious heritage—from Scandinavia to Australia. You find your Communist parties have either taken over or represent very strong open movements in countries whose religious heritage has not stressed the freedom of the individual under God as against ecclesiastical and political control.

Critic: That seems to be the situation now, all right. But I'm worried about one thing, and that is that while countries with a strong religious tradition of individual decision and responsibility display certain capacities, there is still another threat that always faces them which might make them fall to the cold organized efficiency of Communism in the long run, and that is the threat of anarchy. With everybody making up his own mind about everything, it may be very hard for countries to stay organized effectively.

Exponent: These countries to which you refer have on the whole been successful in maintaining themselves as against the onslaughts of their enemies. But I think I can also answer you in terms of this "long run" that you are concerned about. First of all, a culture with a principle of self-criticism at the heart of its basic religious influence is more likely to avoid the pitfalls and hazards to which an uncritical point of view inevitably leads a nation. A nation or a church which demands conformity and silences criticism is really the loser in the long run. But second, we're talking about one authority that does remain and is the basis of the freedom from other author-ities, namely, the allegiance to God. We mean, when we say this, the *same* God, and it is to be assumed, and it certainly seems to work out in history in the large, that the God of nations who is also the God of the individual speaks to the hearts of individuals in a way that they can be moved to co-operate freely for the maintenance of their common life without being forced into an authoritarian way. It is on this hope that our nation was founded, and this democratic fulfillment is one of the finest flowers of the roots of Christian belief. It is the only true and abiding basis of individual freedom.

CHAPTER TEN

"Should Christians in democracies have fellow-ship with Church leaders from behind the Iron Curtain?"

CRITIC: Not too long ago I read in the papers that delegates came from all over the world for the Assembly of the World Council of Churches at Evanston. I think the World Council is a fine thing and I am glad that the representation in its meeting is wide but there was one thing that disturbed me. A number of delegates came from countries that are behind the Iron Curtain, and it had been pointed out by certain groups in our country that these delegates had accepted, conformed to, and might even have been collaborating with, the Communist regime. Now I wonder if it was a good thing for them to be allowed to come into our country to participate in this meeting.

Exponent: You don't think these Churchmen were functioning as Communist spies while they were over here, do you?

Critic: No, I don't really think that. But I do have some serious questions about the whole thing. How can we have real Christian fellowship with people that are tied in with the Communists? How can they be regarded as true Christians at all? After all, Communism is atheistic.

Exponent: Communism is atheistic, of course, but I have no evidence that any of these Churchmen who came had accepted the dogmas of Communism. It is possible for people to be in favor of a socialistic economic system or even an authoritarian governmental system and still not accept the doctrinaire beliefs which underlie the aims of the Marxists.

Critic: Even so, we Americans are opposed to Communism on any level. We believe in capitalism in economics and democracy in government.

Exponent: You speak of loyalty to our way of life, but your complaint about these delegates is that they were being loyal to their countries. If loyalty to one's country and its way of life is the primary thing in life, these people would eminently qualify—at least if they are as related to Communism as you think they are. After all, we receive visitors from Spain, which has a way of government and an official practice of religious regimentation which is far out of line with what we endorse here. I don't think we have to agree with all the ideas of people that we are willing to talk with.

Critic: No, we don't have to agree with all the ideas of people whom we talk with, but certain things are basic to Christian thought, and I would suggest that free enterprise is one of them. Now these people openly criticize our capitalistic system.

Exponent: Well, the World Council of Churches, meeting in Amsterdam some time back, criticized both Communism and capitalism with a sort of "plague on both your houses."

Critic: That was very disturbing to a good many people over here too.

Exponent: Yes, I know, there are many in America who would like to have seen a condemnation of Communism—which the Council did come through with, without any question—and then a strong pat on the back for our American capitalism. But actually the Church cannot endorse unqualifiedly any economic system. Its job is to keep all the doings of men under judgment and under criticism.

Critic: But isn't the criticism of capitalism un-American?

Exponent: Not at all. Now, I'm for the free enterprise system; but the fact is that it has always been under criticism in this country. That's why it has undergone so many revisions. After all, the capitalism of, say, the eighteen-nineties is quite different from the capitalism of today. There is no one, or at least there are very few, who are so die-hard or right-wing that he would like things to be just as they were then. The regulation of the hours of work, the prohibition of child labor, the place of collective bargaining—all these things represent revisions of an untrammeled free enterprise system which have come from criticism—and quite loyal criticism—right within our own country. The Church has often been in the forefront of this criticism.

Critic: Your phrase "loyal criticism" interests me ——

Exponent: This raises a whole subject which we at least ought to touch on for a moment. There was growing for a while in this country, as you know, a new doctrine which arose in part from our fear of Communism and in part from the demagoguery of certain persons in public life. This new doctrine was that if you dissent at all from the *status quo* in the economic order, or if you become part of any movement to change things in any field, then this non-conformity automatically makes you un-American. More than that, if you protest against this new doctrine of conformity itself, you are un-American too.

Critic: Well, I can agree with you on that point, and I see what you mean, but this is quite apart from what our attitude should be toward a world movement which is seeking to destroy the Churches and undermine the whole religious foundation of our common life.

Exponent: Yes, that does raise a different problem. But before we move on to that problem I would like to remind you that some of these demagogues of conformity in our land tried pretty hard to undermine the confidence of people in the *Protestant* Churches at least, and to this degree were serving one of the well-known purposes of the Communists that these demagogues are supposed to be opposing. But be that as it may, there is no question in my mind that Communism is out to destroy the Churches. They may temporize, they may even seek to use the ecclesiastical machinery for their own ends, but in the long run they do see the Church as an enemy of all that they stand for.

Critic: Don't the Christian leaders in these countries see this?

Exponent: They certainly do. It is hardly lost on them. On the other hand, it is possible for them to conceive that conditions have been so bad under previous regimes (we must remember, for example, that Communism has followed a Nazi or, in some cases, virtually a feudal regime) that certain gains might come into the life of the people—a better distribution of land, better public order, a better standard of living and so forth, under a regime run even by people who believe the exact opposite about religion. Now we don't think that this is so—that in the long run these regimes will be good for these countries; but we can't say that these people aren't Christians just because they may think that this is so.

Critic: But what about this basic attack on the Churches themselves?

Exponent: Well, there I think we have to try to put ourselves in the position of the Christian leaders in those countries. Naturally, they would prefer to have a regime that was friendly to Christianity, regardless of what the economics or political structure might be, but *that* they don't have. Now they have the choice of putting up with this situation and being enabled to continue the life of their Churches and their influence upon individual souls—which you and I have agreed all along in these discussions is the primary job of the Church—or to make an open break and lose that basic opportunity.

Critic: That's just plain compromise, isn't it?

Exponent: It could be, under one set of motives. Under another set it might be instead of worldly compromise and a "saving of their skins" as it were, a real effort to exist under difficult conditions so that the life of the Church might continue to be an influence—perhaps even upon those with atheistic beliefs. The hope is that people can be brought to see that it is possible to have an ordered and fair society on *Christian* presuppositions. Now I am not able to say that the motives of all these leaders is in every case a self-sacrificing, a painful effort to try to make the best of a situation so that the life of the Church may continue, or whether it is some kind of time-serving out of fear or out of hope of getting ahead. On the other hand, you can't make that judgment either; only God can. I think it is important for us at this point simply to recognize that this same conduct—whether we might agree with its wisdom or not—can be the one thing or the other thing, but we have to leave it to God to judge. And one thing I think that might well give some of these Church leaders a certain humility in the face of the Communist onslaught is that the very existence of Communism in these countries and of large Communist parties in certain others, is in itself a judgment on the Christian society and the Church which has been complacent in the face of the failure to meet certain pressing problems of poverty and housing—and of the freedom of the individual, for that matter. In a sense, "the Assyrians are the rod of God," as the Bible tells us.

Critic: Yes, there is much in what you say. But don't you think that certain liberal Christians in this country have been inclined to beat themselves and their compatriots over the head because of our shortcomings and at the same time have been rather naive about excusing in an uncritical way the shortcomings of some of the Communist regimes.

Exponent: I agree with you, but before I get into that I would like to remind you that our Lord seemed to be a little more fond of the publican than the pharisee. All of us can do with a good deal of self-criticism from whatever source it comes, even if it comes from an alien source. But it is true that in the Church's educational task it has got to be very realistic and direct its main shots against what is the main enemy. While our capitalist structure needs constant attention and a critical view from the Church, *Communism* as a whole world-view, which would engulf everything we hold dear, has to be criticized not only in terms of its economic and political results but constantly in terms of its basic ideology and what it does to the souls of men, and the destruction it will wreak upon Christian civilization throughout the world. I think these days there are very few Church leaders who are blind to this necessity and very few who now do take an uncritical view of what is going on behind the Iron Curtain.

Critic: But the same isn't necessarily true of those Churchmen who are behind the Iron Curtain. Far from just putting up with Communism, it seems to me that they've been joining in the cause with enthusiasm and have been applauding the Communist way of life. And in all this they've certainly encouraged Communism by their apparent moral approval.

Exponent: That puts it a little strong, I think. But even if we can say that they are apparently loyal to the regime in their own countries, at the same time their main work is spreading the Christian Gospel and deepening the Christian faith of the people in those countries. But actually, isn't this the only chance we have to change the regime at all: by so encouraging Christian ideas that the people will be impatient with a regime which makes it impossible for those ideas to be put into effect?

Critic: That seems rather long-range and remote in the face of the crisis that we have upon us right now.

Exponent: It is long-range, and yet what other alternative is there? Short of an extermination by atomic warfare which none of us want, there is no other avenue of hope actually open except the hope that there will be internal resistance against the Communist regime in these countries, and I know of no basis of laying the foundation for this other than the deepening of the Christian life of the people and the new generation coming on.

Critic: Well, there's one problem with all this that bothers me. You're assuming that these people can reason their way from general Christian principles to a democratic way of life. Wouldn't it be much more direct and effective if we just came right to the point and taught them the elements of the democratic way of life right now? It seems to me that we'd do better to put all our weight behind the aggressive measures which have been taken by the Crusade for Free Europe and the Voice of America than to be temporizing with these Christian leaders that are tinged with the Communist propaganda.

Exponent: All those efforts were very useful, I'm sure, but they have one limitation that we shouldn't overlook: They are pretty clearly labeled "Made in U.S.A." and by that very fact unacceptable to many people taught by their Communist masters to hate us and to be suspicious of us. In any case, no country wants to feel that it is taking over lock, stock, and barrel the way of life of another country that claims to be superior. The real hope is that the roots of Christian belief right within their own land can bring forth the fruitage of a thirst for

God and for freedom which will be impatient with atheistic Communism or any form of authoritarianism. In other words, I admit that this may be long-range, but I know of nothing that would be more effective.

Critic: Aren't you forgetting one very important thing, and that is that behind the Iron Curtain there are brave people who are engaged in a quiet but persistent secret opposition to the Communist order? Now if we give public recognition or support to these fellow travelers, aren't we being unfair to the people that are really working against the Communist way of life in our interests?

Exponent: Obviously, those who are in actual positive resistance in an underground way represent one important approach. On the other hand, by that very fact they are not able to serve in the particularly responsible positions that the leaders of the Church hold in these countries. And in the case of the latter, in order to maintain public worship and continue to influence their flocks, they may not be able to express their resistance in such direct terms. They express it rather in terms of continuing the positive teaching of belief in God and the implications of that belief as to what human life should be like in society.

Critic: But how can you reconcile their teachings about belief in God and the so-called Christian way of life with their support of such obvious falsehoods as the germ-warfare charges and the hypocrisy of the ersatz Communist peace campaigns?

Exponent: I don't see a problem there. I was not impressed by the germ-warfare charges and I know you weren't: but here we're dealing with a question of fact, not a question of doctrine or belief. Now the likelihood that people will believe certain facts depends in good measure upon what sort of propaganda they've been fed. When the Iron Curtain people say that germs were used and America says they weren't, what is there in Christian revelation which decides *that* question for these Churchmen beyond the Iron Curtain?

Critic: But by allowing these people to come here and participate in the World Council meeting, didn't we give them just the opportunity they wanted to spread this kind of nonsense?

Exponent: You're assuming that these Christians beyond the Iron Curtain do want to spread this kind of nonsense. I have no reason to believe that any number of them even believe it. We didn't hear any speeches from them in the World Council of Churches on the alleged American use of germ warfare. But even so, there are even Americans who happened to think that we used germ warfare and since again that's a question of fact, they were not forbidden from so thinking. Again, I think these people were dead wrong and naive indeed, but my point is that this country is big enough and strong enough to sustain the possibility of some people stating such an opinion within its borders. I doubt very much if many people would have been convinced or polluted intellectually on this point in our country even if some delegate to the World Council of Churches from behind the Iron Curtain had gone ahead and made such a charge.

But what you're overlooking is that this matter of communication is a two way street. Presumably, when these delegates were here, they saw something of our way of life and the accustomed freedoms that we value, and were in conversation with people who were in a good position to answer charges of this sort, and also to persuade them of the fallacy of Communism—even along economic and political lines, as well as strengthening the conviction of these people that they already hold against the atheistic doctrines of Communism. Again, I've got enough trust in America and its way of life to believe that it presents a winsome and attractive picture to these people.

Critic: The way you put it, it would appear that their own governments should have been more worried about their coming to us that we should have been worried about letting them in.

Exponent: Exactly. I personally feel that it was a real opportunity.

Critic: But an opportunity with a risk.

Exponent: Well, if you mean by risk that they might have said some things persuading our people to be favorable to the Communists, I must say that I do not regard that as a very great risk. As a matter of fact, if I thought it were a great risk, I would examine myself on how much confidence I really had in the claims of our position and the justification for our place in the world. I am very optimistic about the attractiveness of our way of life and the soundness of our position. If by risk you mean that they might have used their time, instead of attending meetings and discussion groups, in engaging in espionage, I think this too implies that we have an inadequate system for protecting ourselves against this sort of thing, especially since these people were well known and their headquarters while here were quite specifically defined.

More than all of this, I think our people should be heartened as to the confidence we have in ourselves, and the breadth of freedom we in fact allow, to actually see the picture of people of radically different points of view being allowed to come to this country to express themselves and to be answered—where appropriate—by exponents of our free way of life, and at the same time to know that underneath it all, there is the common conviction of belief in God and loyalty to the Kingdom of God, however much difference there may be in the thinking of exponents of these two positions as to how the Kingdom of God is best expressed in the actual conditions of society. I say this with no wavering as to my conviction and your conviction about the merits of the free way of life. It is because of my confidence in the free way of life that I believe that we had more to gain than lose by bringing into the orbit of discussion with us, under the auspices of a group devoted to the Lordship of Christ, those who had been influenced in other directions due to the tragic extension of the Iron Curtain to their countries. It was an opportunity for us to be dealing with persons from behind the Iron Curtain who were here to affirm with us that when all is said and done the theme of the Assembly is the truth, that Christ is the Hope of the World.

CHAPTER ELEVEN

"What is the use of the World Council of Churches, with all the Churches believing different things?"

CRITIC: For some time I've been very much concerned with this matter of the unity of the various denominations. We've observed already that the divided Church speaks with too uncertain a voice in the face of many of the serious problems facing the world today. Now, as I have observed the way the World Council of Churches and its predecessor movements have carried on their discussions over many decades now, I've come to wonder about the effectiveness of their way of dealing with the problem of unity. Wouldn't it be better if instead of going into long and involved theological discussions of the differences between different Churches, the Churches just faced up to the problem and got together on the minimum essentials of the faith and went ahead and united? Actually, all of this theological discussion just magnifies differences rather than creating the unity that we really need.

Exponent: Actually, the leaders in the ecumenical

movement have all along been just as concerned for Church unity in the world as you are. But the question is the best way to achieve Church unity. I'd like to take the time to tell a little story here.

There were two bishops on a platform at some large event, and one of the bishops said to the other, "I think that we ought to be chatting and appearing to be friendly up here because of the nature of this gathering and also because, Bishop, we do worship the same Lord."

Critic: What did the other one say?

Exponent: He said, "Yes, Bishop, we do: you in your way, and I in His."

Obviously, that isn't the way that we're going to get Church unity.

Critic: Well, that's precisely why I propose that we forget about our theological differences and get together on the minimum essentials that make unity possible.

Exponent: There are two difficulties here. The first is one which I think perhaps could in time be surmounted: the various denominations actually do differ sometimes in regard to what they think is essential. But there is a second difficulty that I think lies more at the basis of the kinds of discussion the World Council of Churches has had at the Amsterdam and Lund conferences and more recently at Evanston. I mean this: each of the great traditions has stood for emphases and insights about the meaning of Christian faith and life which are not only important to the members of that group, but which can be very fruitful in deepening the religious experience and stimulating the ethical action of all other Christians as well. If we forget about these, then everybody is the poorer. For example, wherever the Reformed, or Presbyterian, tradition is being itself, we get a great emphasis on the absolute sovereignty of God, the sense that in every relationship it's always God first, man second. This is a note that is very important as men over and over again try to "bootstrap" themselves out of their problems. And it is out of this basic motif that the idea we often associate with the Presbyterians—predestination—stems. Understood properly, this says something important to the whole of the Christian world.

Critic: This is interesting. Tell me about the Lutherans then. What is their distinctive contribution?

Exponent: My experience with Lutherans is that if you go into a Lutheran church almost any Sunday, you are apt in one form or another to hear a sermon on justification by grace through faith, and I might say that if you are going to have a standard message, that's a good one to have. Right at the center of the problem of human personality is the problem of how a man can have self-criticism and also have self-acceptance. The answer to this is finally found in what the doctrine of justification is trying to tell us: that our standing with God, and thus our standing with ourselves, doesn't rest upon our own goodness but upon God's accepting us though unacceptable, thus giving us the motive of thanksgiving as a basis of becoming more acceptable. This, again, is something so easily forgotten in a sort of minimal or "Golden Rule" Christianity that so many advocate as the basis of a simple getting together.

Critic: I realize that the Lutheran emphasis on justification is pretty important; but have the Methodists, for example, anything distinctive to add to that?

Exponent: Yes. Starting with this emphasis that I've just outlined, the Methodists have a heightened sense of the consequences of this whole experience. They stress that when a man gets religion, something is really supposed to happen in his life, and not only in his own life but in the life of society around him; and out of this has come a great deal of the social zeal of Methodism. In other words, the sanctification of personal and corporate life that is to follow from justification has been a consistent emphasis with them.

Critic: Well, that's important too. But I've never seen anything especially distinctive about the Congregational churches.

Exponent: Oh yes, there is. There's a strong witness to the fact that the Church is the people and that the people are the Church. You feel this especially in many New England communities which are one-church towns. You certainly feel the power of "the priesthood of all believers."

Critic: Let's take that point that you just mentioned.

You don't mean to say that other Churches don't believe that too?

Exponent: As a matter of fact they do, and this is true of all the distinctive points I've mentioned, whether it be the sovereignty of God, or justification, or sanctification, or the ministry of the laity. But while in theory we all hold to these things and in a measure demonstrate them in our traditions, certain particular groups have, we might say, made a specialty of keeping them before us, and have often done a much better job in demonstrating their implications than the rest of us have.

Critic: I see this in connection with these major groups you've mentioned, each of which has an established tradition. But here in America we have many Churches of quite a different kind. We have scores of small sects and Churches that can't possibly all have something distinctive to tell us.

Exponent: Actually, the Churches to which you're referring do have something distinctive to tell us. In Church history we generally make a distinction between Churches, to which everybody pretty much belongs that's born into them, and sects, which people make an adult decision to come into. And these latter groups generally represent some kind of a "come-outer" movement. In times past, where things were lax in the particular group from which they came, they represented people who were very eager to re-establish their common life in a purified form, and to mark themselves off from the world around them. Roger Williams' movement is an example of this, and the most conspicuous group of this type, of course, is the Baptists. But whether it be a large group of this sort, or a very small group, all these Churches can remind us of what the very word "sect" means: It means a good thing, "cut off." It means that being a Christian should make you a marked man, and becoming a Christian represents a decision to be different. That, too, is something that we would want to be quite paramount in the coming great Church, set as it would be in the midst of a secular world.

Critic: We certainly can't limit the coming great Church to Protestants. What abiding contributions can we expect from the Roman Catholic Church, for example?

Exponent: Well now in discussing each of these traditions, it's only possible to pick out one motif or two as illustrative of what a particular group is holding before the rest of us in the world by way of a special witness. But certainly an obvious one for the Roman Catholic Church would be that sense of loyalty and discipline without which the Church never can become an effective instrument in the world. While this is not true in all countries throughout the world, certainly in America an evident witness is made by Roman Catholics by the loyalty with which they attend church and put their Church first, ahead of lesser considerations. For example, when Protestants have house guests for a weekend, they are apt to excuse themselves from going to church, whereas the Roman Catholic hosts are likely to say, "Here is the Sunday paper. We'll be back from church at such-and-such an hour," and perhaps throw in, "Come along with us if you like."

Critic: There is a large group of Churches very much involved in the ecumenical movement which don't fit into any of the pictures you've drawn. Those are the Eastern Orthodox Churches.

Exponent: Certainly one thing strikes a stranger to their tradition immediately, and that is the sense of, we might say, holy mystery, by which there is a recognition that we worship God through a cloud. And yet, unlike agnostics and some liberal Protestants, they don't just avoid religious realities because they know they can't fully grasp them this side of the grave, but maintain a worshiping relationship even through the cloud. This is a great note which should have a large part in our theological thinking and in our worship.

Critic: Are you too shy to say a good word about the tradition with which we're both connected, the Episcopal Church?

Exponent: No, not at all. One motif, for example, of the Anglican heritage is the vivid sense of the communion of saints, the sense of visible continuity which makes the Church an organism and not just a committee, which gives a sense of the actual present reality of the saints of old—their penetrating, as it were, our life and worship—a sort of heavenly rooting section, backing us up in our course here on earth.

Critic: The things that you've been mentioning are all very good and they are good because they are positive things, about which there isn't any serious difference of opinion on the part of the different Churches involved. But there are other things that are held by these different Churches which represent a flat contradiction, and they're held just as firmly as the points that you've mentioned. For example, I might mention the fact that some Churches hold very strongly that Baptism should be strictly a matter for adults, whereas other Churches believe equally strongly in infant Baptism.

Exponent: That's true. One of the purposes of the kind of ecumenical conversations going on under the auspices of the World Council of Churches and elsewhere is to face honestly these very differences and not to minimize the fact of conflict. However, in these conversations there is an eagerness, and properly so, to see what each group is really trying to say and what they're really witnessing to by their insistence upon their position. The matter of Baptism is a very good example of this because, actually, both sides of that contradiction are saying something important. The idea of adult Baptism stresses the importance of mature, free decision to be a Christian, as marking oneself off from the world. On the other hand, infant Baptism stands for something important too. It witnesses to the reality of the Christian family and the fact that God and His grace are reaching even little ones as they grow into appreciation and responsiveness to grace, which is the aim of the whole process. We could discuss many other such contradictions, but just as a symbol of the way in which opposites may both say something important to us, let me mention the fact that in the West (for instance in the Roman Catholic, Anglican, and Lutheran Churches) red is used as the proper color for Whitsunday or Pentecost, and in the Eastern Church green is used.

Critic: They certainly are opposites, as anyone that has seen a traffic light knows.

Exponent: Yes, but see what they mean. The West uses red to emphasize the fact that the Holy Spirit comes, as it were, in tongues of flame, to fire us into new life. The green means, on the other hand, the growth that comes in the life of the individual and of the Church through the steady, reliable operation of the Holy Spirit. Now both things are true, though the colors be opposite.

Critic: I can see that both thoughts are very inspiring. That sort of thing isn't going to keep us apart in the long run. But there are other things that have an effect on the life of the Churches that we haven't mentioned. These are such things as sociological differences that have developed in the course of the history of the Churches. Some Churches seem to be identified with certain social and economic groups, and other Churches with others, and these groups in many cases are associ ated with different educational levels, different social customs. Now don't these things keep the Churches apart perhaps even more than theological differences? I know from my own experience that in many a town in this country the church divisions have little or nothing to do with theology. People go to one church or the other simply on the basis of the traditions of their forebears or depending upon how much they feel at home with the kind of people that they find there.

Exponent: This is a very considerable factor, I agree. But I have a feeling that there is hope in this regard and that the sociological factors will be less and less as time goes on, simply because something's been happening to our society as a whole. There has been much more of a mobility of population and a shift in social classes and a more widespread availability of education and other opportunities. Thus the hard and fast lines of class groupings and economic and educational groupings are breaking down. This in itself is bound to give various Church people an experience of the Church life of their neighbors and open up to them a possibility of making independent judgments about the particular part of a divided Christendom they want to work through.

Critic: You mentioned that this mobility has provided more opportunities for people to get to know how other people worship. Doesn't this really bring us to the heart of the matter? The things that keep people apart are very likely to be visible differences in ways of wor-

ship that make them feel strange or uncomfortable rather
than the doctrinal matters that you were mentioning
earlier. For most people, doesn't church really mean the
eleven o'clock Sunday morning experience?

Exponent: I am glad you've raised this because it's
right here that I think there is the greatest hopefulness
on the horizon. All of the Churches in one way or
another have been stirred by a movement designed not
only to capture more obviously the great continuous religious heritage of worship but also to make the ways
of worship more relevant in contemporary terms to the
whole task of the Church in life in this world. Here we
are being more and more drawn together in our ways of
worship, and the self-criticism of our particular traditions is making us more open to seeing what lies behind
the way other people worship. We may find it's in the
realm of worship finally, more than in the realm of doctrine, that Church unity really will come.

Critic: Well, that is encouraging, especially in the
light of something that really bothered me a good bit
recently. While there has been this great increase in
ecumenical interest among the Churches, there has been
at the same time, it seems to me, a growing sense of individual denominational loyalties. Sometimes this has
even been the by-product of mergers between certain
denominational groups that had been separated. When
they merge, they become big, and when they become
big, they become very much aware of their distinctive-

ness and have less interest, really, in the problem of Church unity.

Exponent: Paradoxical as it may seem, I think the concurrence of these two movements, that is, greater ecumenical concern and deeper denominational self-consciousness, all adds up to a pretty good result when we consider how unity is really going to have to come. It is true that the Methodists are becoming more Methodist and are looking back to their roots—to John Wesley and his distinctive emphases; the Presbyterians and the Reformed are becoming more Calvinistic, really trying to grasp what Calvin's basic motifs were; and the same with the Lutherans, and so forth. And while that may look like the increasing of divisiveness, actually, as each group digs down to its own foundations, we find that at that point we are more firmly united upon the essential things the Church has to say to the world today than at any other point. Though in their own times Luther and Calvin and Wesley and Hooker may have sounded at variance with each other, as we look back upon them from the perspective of history they are very much closer to each other than our present modern denominational expressions have become, and we are finding back there a great seedbed of present unity in ideas and inspiration.

What makes the Churches aware of the unity that's involved in this searching deeper in their own traditions, what keeps the traditional self-consciousness from becoming a threat, is that there is an opportunity now in the world for constant conversation, and this is perhaps the greatest advantage of the World Council of Churches, not only in its great gatherings, but in the continuing day-to-day work of its committees and reports. The fact is that when each group gets down deep enough in its own heritage—no matter what issues may have been posed in the particular historical time—one thing emerges as pre-eminent, namely, that it is Christ that is the hope of the world. Our salvation will not be of men's doing alone, and the Kingdom will not be brought in by merely astute committee work. Our final trust and reliance must be in the King of the Kingdom, who in His own good time, as we receive Him in our hearts and in our corporate and community life, will bring the reign of peace and the joy of fulfillment. This will be the heart of the message of the coming great Church: "Christ the Hope of the World."